Sketching and Rendering

for Design Presentations

Sketching and Rendering
for Design Presentations

Janet Shen   Theodore D. Walker

 VAN NOSTRAND REINHOLD
New York

Copyright © 1992 by Van Nostrand Reinhold
Library of Congress Catalog Card Number 92–3369
ISBN 0-442-00414-1

Printed in the United States of America

Van Nostrand Reinhold
115 Fifth Avenue
New York, New York 10003

Chapman and Hall
2-6 Boundary Row
London, SE1 8HN, England

Thomas Nelson Australia
102 Dodds Street
South Melbourne, Victoria 3205, Australia

Nelson Canada
1120 Birchmount Road
Scarborough, Ontario MIK 5G4, Canada

16 15 14 13 12 11 10 9 8 7 6 5 4 3 2 1

Library of Congress Cataloging-in-Publication Data

Shen, Janet, 1936-
    Sketching and rendering for design presentations / Janet Shen and
Theodore D. Walker.
        p.   cm.
    Includes index.
    ISBN 0-442-00414-1
    1. Architecture—Presentation drawings.   2. Architectural drawing—
—Technique.   3. Architectural rendering—Technique.   I. Walker,
Theodore D.   II.   Title.
NA2714.S53   1992
720'.28'4—dc20   92–3369
                                                              CIP

CONTENTS

ACKNOWLEDGMENTS

The authors gratefully acknowledge the generosity of the following individuals and firms who granted permission for us to use their work or projects in this book.

Mr. and Mrs. Robert Brooks
Browning Day Mullins Dierdorf, Inc.
A. E. Bye
Captur Company
Griskells Smith Architects, Ltd.
Hansen Lind Meyer, Inc.
State of Illinois Tollway Authority
Lannert Group/St. Charles Park District
Mr. and Mrs. Marsh McMahon
Perkins & Will International
Perkins & Will, Inc.
Planning Resource, Inc.
Shen & Associates, Inc.
Walsh, Higgins & Company

INTRODUCTION

In recent years there has been increasing demand for illustrators who are skilled in sketching and rendering. These skills are required to produce high quality presentations for the design professions.

This book provides some of the basic knowledge of perspective construction and rendering techniques helpful to the beginner. It also will serve as a "quick" reference for those who may have had some of the basics previously. Many of the examples and rendering techniques illustrated will be useful to those who are experienced.

After acquiring a knowledge of the basics, it takes practice, observing and developing to achieve accuracy, proficiency, and style in sketching and rendering. Freehand sketching during the design process and during idle moments can be very helpful in developing skills. Such an individual can become conscious of scale and will improve composition abilities. Observing the work of others is also profitable. One can study photographs and make sketches from them as another means of observing and developing skills. Many photographs have been provided in this book for that purpose.

The development of one's own style is the goal of nearly every illustrator. This may be difficult to achieve at first, but as you become skilled and confident in your technique, the style will emerge.

Sketching and rendering is a visual activity. The final illustration is in pictorial or visual form. Words cannot adequately express the "mood" or "feel" that can be created in an illustration or work of art. Even though we have done our best to describe the skills and techniques involved in sketching and rendering, the illustrations in this book speak louder than the words, and are the best source of information.

The primary intent of the illustrating approach we are describing is to convey the design intent of the project to the client. Sketching and rendering are powerful marketing tools for the designer as they help a client to visualize what he is getting for his money, early in the design phase.

According to Allen Hurlburt in his book, *The Design Concept*, the creative process can be generally divided into four stages: analyzing, incubation, inspiration, and verification. From time to time during the design process, the designer needs to explore ideas. One way of visualizing the design concept is in three dimensional form. Building a scale model is one way, though time consuming and expensive. The better approach is through perspective sketching. This is especially desirable during the inspiration and verification stages or phases. Sketching enables the designer to explore the possibilities and check the feasibility of his/her ideas in a very short period of time at any scale. Anyone who acquires the basic skills of sketching and rendering will find their design skills greatly enhanced.

This book is divided into five sections. Section I describes and illustrates perspective theory and construction. Section II covers composition while Section III demonstrates rendering techniques. Section IV provides some step-by-step examples, and Section V is a collection of perspectives with various forms, view points, and techniques that hopefully will cover most situations usually encountered in perspective illustration.

1

PERSPECTIVE THEORY
and CONSTRUCTION

PRE-CONSIDERATIONS—GETTING STARTED

The process of preparing an illustration for a design presentation is similar to a painting being done by an artist. Although the objectives are slightly different, the principles are much the same. It involves conscious preplanning from the beginning. The following items are all interrelated and need to be considered before you begin. This is especially important for beginners. As you practice and gain experience, the planning will become more subconscious and natural.

1. **View selection**: The most important consideration in preparing an illustration involves selecting the view point from which the object will be seen. This may be a space, a building, or a planting area. It would be beneficial to discuss this with any other designers involved in the project, or the client, during the initial meetings. The usual intent is to express the most dramatic and effective view. An artist (illustrator or designer) should be able to draw quick freehand sketches and communicate with the client, and to be able to make recommendations and judgments. Many times a complicated project will require more than one view or illustration, such as an exterior eye level close-up of a space as well as an aerial view of the overall area of the project.

2. **Time schedule:** Unfortunately, for most illustration projects, time is usually limited. The entire process involving the collection of information, roughouts, revisions, approval of the line base, reproduction and meetings all need to fit into the time schedule. After gaining some experience you can quite often roughly estimate the hours needed for each of these steps.

3. **Size required:** The size of the drawing is largely based upon the illustrator's convenience, his/her choice of composition and artistic judgment. He/she also determines whether it will be a vertical, horizontal or square picture. By using different scales, reduction or enlargement of the base layout, the drawing can be of

any size. If the final drawing is to be published, the original size should be in proportion with the layout. The size of the drawing has a direct effect on the time required. A larger drawing tends to have more detail thus requiring more time than a small drawing.

4. **Reproduction method:** It is important to plan ahead as the media used dictates the medium used for reproduction, and thus the time required. For instance, a drawing on vellum or mylar can be directly printed on bond paper or card stock, and the final rendering applied. It also can be printed on photographic paper through an outside service, which may require an additional two days. Transferring base line drawings by graphite paper to an art board or by a special photographic process differ in cost and time, which needs consideration.

5. **Finish technique**: Generally speaking each illustrator has his/her own style. They typically repeat the same technique with minor variation to achieve special effects. The finish technique is directly related to the time required to complete the task. For example, a freehand line drawing with color wash is simple and time saving. On the other hand, a watercolor or air brush is time consuming.

PREPARATION REQUIREMENTS

1. **Site Plan**: A plot plan or site plan is needed that indicates all of the features on the site or surrounding area, which are above ground. This includes such things as trees, buildings, walks, steps, and so forth. (See Figure 1.1)

2. **Grading Plan**: In many cases the grading plan is combined with the site plan in one drawing. It shows the land form, whether the property is a rolling ground surface, or developed with relatively flat surfaces, steps, walls, and so forth. From it, we will be able to interpolate to a three dimensional drawing. (See Figure 1.2)

3. **Planting Plan**: Includes the location of all existing and proposed planting. (See Figures 1.3 and 1.4)

4. **Ground Floor Plan:** This plan illustrates the proposed building(s). The floor plan provides you with the location of windows, doors, pillars, and other building features that will be important for your illustration. (See Figure 1.5)

5. **Elevations, Sections and Details**: They provide information about height, and help you with angles, curves, recesses, and protrusions. From these drawings you will gather information about the materials being used in the building, which will help you to illustrate them correctly. (See Figures 1.6 and 1.7)

6. **Aerial and Site Photos**: It helps to obtain site photos and sometimes an aerial photo to provide additional information that may not be available on the drawings listed above. Photos provide the appearance of the surroundings of the site, which will add more realism to your illustration. (See samples in Section 4)

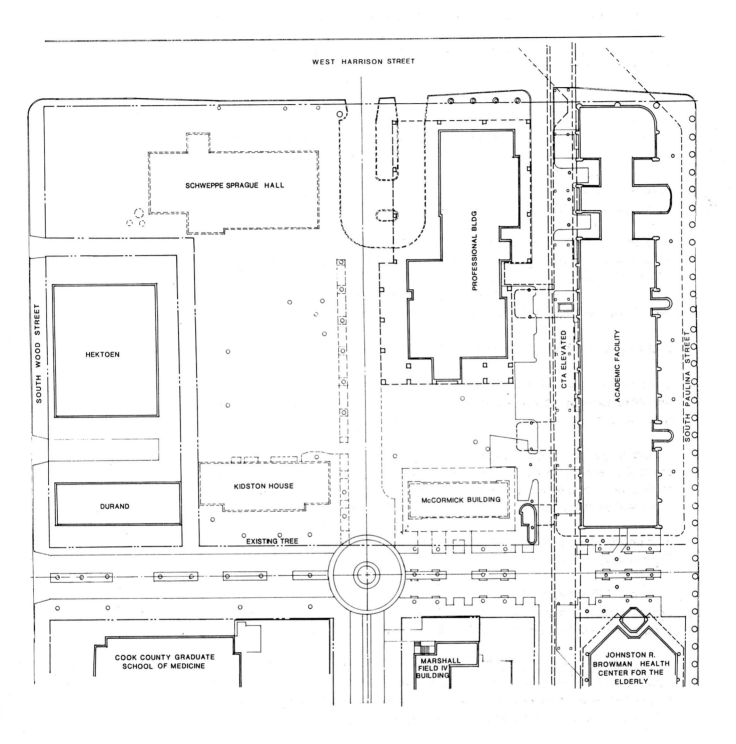

WEST HARRISON STREET

SOUTH WOOD STREET

SCHWEPPE SPRAGUE HALL

HEKTOEN

DURAND

KIDSTON HOUSE

EXISTING TREE

PROFESSIONAL BLDG

McCORMICK BUILDING

CTA ELEVATED

ACADEMIC FACILITY

SOUTH PAULINA STREET

COOK COUNTY GRADUATE
SCHOOL OF MEDICINE

MARSHALL
FIELD IV
BUILDING

JOHNSTON R.
BROWMAN HEALTH
CENTER FOR THE
ELDERLY

EXISTING CAMPUS

0   32   64   128

Fig. 1.1 *A Site Plan (or plot plan)*

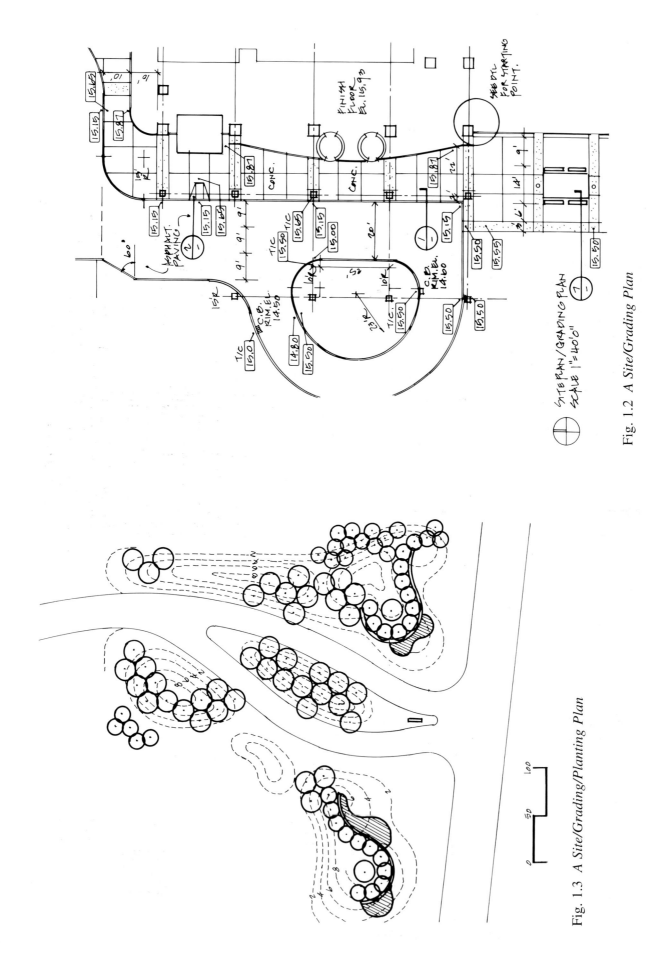

Fig. 1.2 A Site/Grading Plan

Fig. 1.3 A Site/Grading/Planting Plan

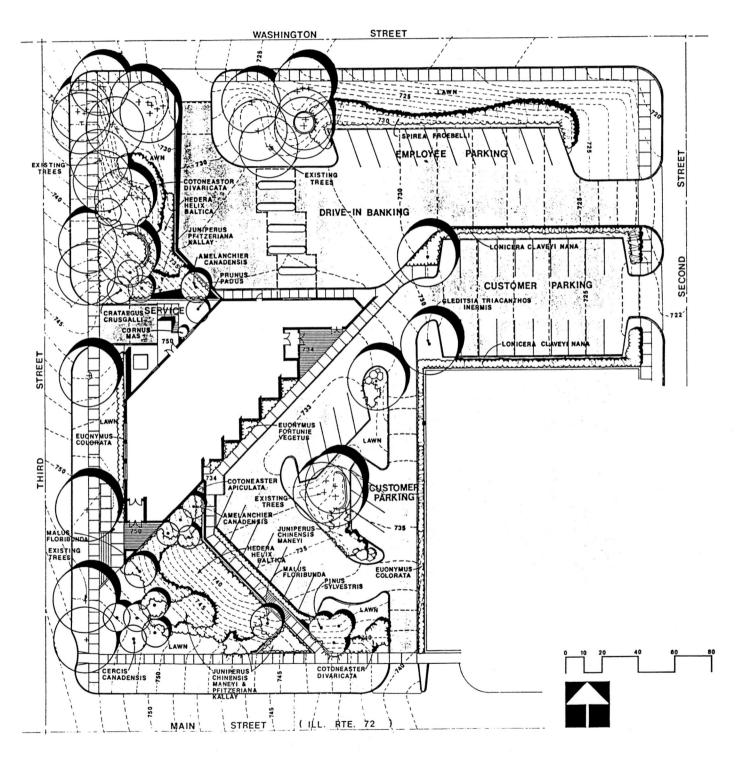

Fig. 1.4 *A Planting Plan*

5

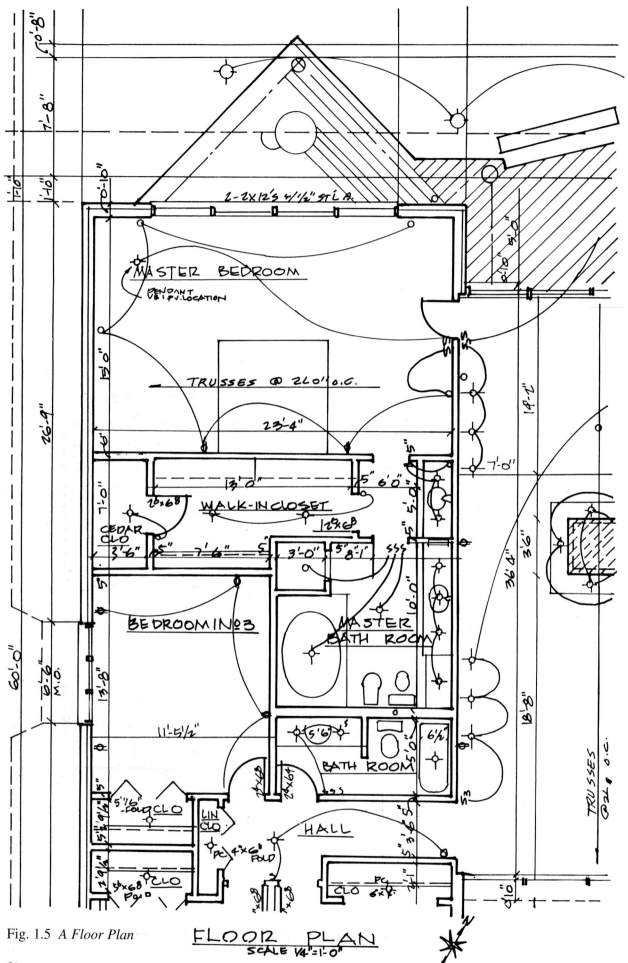

Fig. 1.5 *A Floor Plan*

FLOOR PLAN
SCALE 1/4"=1'-0"

6

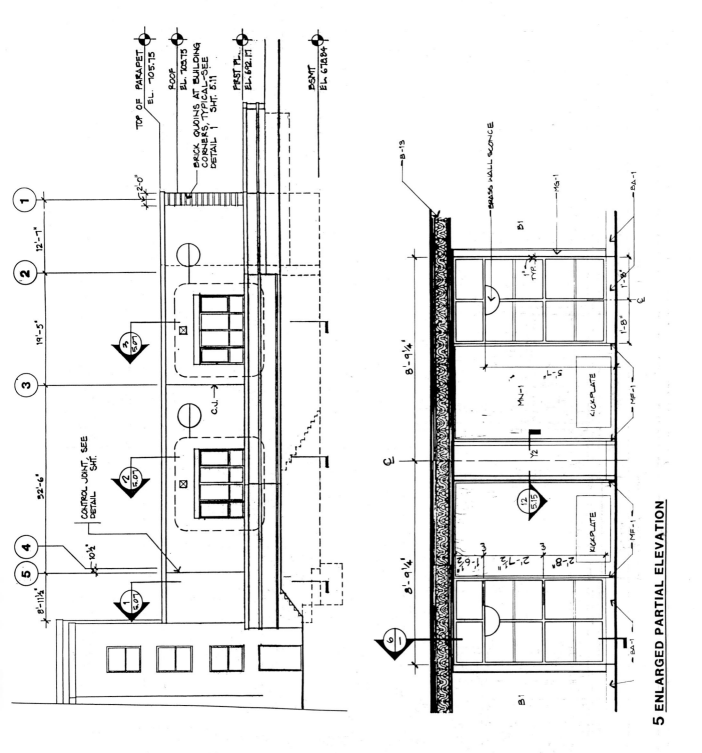

Fig. 1.6 *Building Elevations (exterior, left and interior, right)*

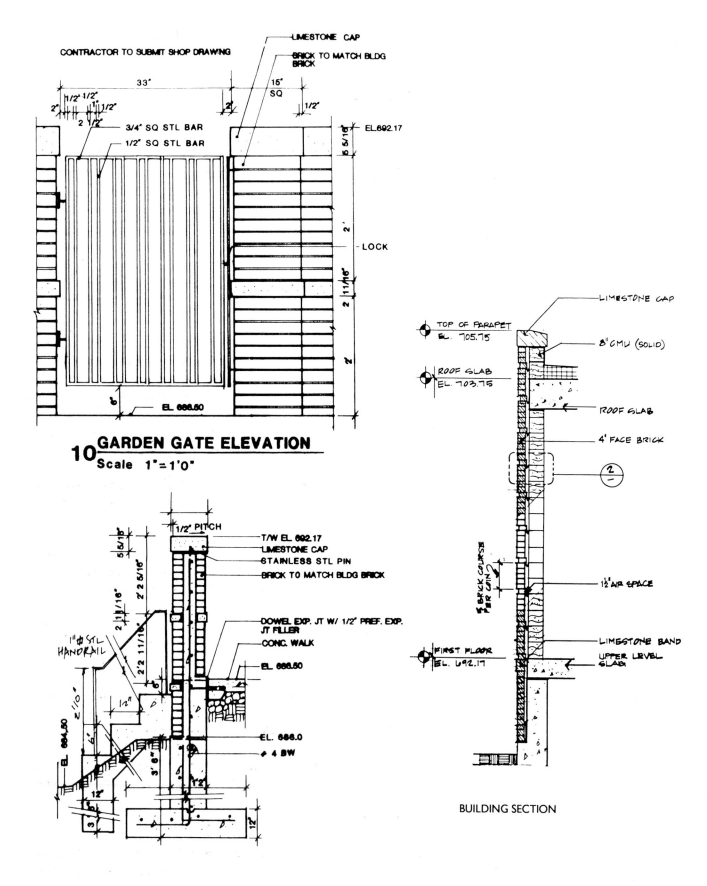

CONTRACTOR TO SUBMIT SHOP DRAWING

LIMESTONE CAP

BRICK TO MATCH BLDG BRICK

33"

15" SQ

3/4" SQ STL BAR

1/2" SQ STL BAR

EL.692.17

LOCK

2'

2' 11/16"

2'

6"

EL. 688.50

10 **GARDEN GATE ELEVATION**
Scale   1"=1'0"

1/2" PITCH

T/W EL. 692.17
LIMESTONE CAP
STAINLESS STL PIN
BRICK TO MATCH BLDG BRICK

DOWEL EXP. JT W/ 1/2" PREF. EXP. JT FILLER
CONC. WALK
EL. 688.50

1"⌀ STL HANDRAIL

2'0"

EL. 684.50

EL. 686.0

4 BW

3' 6"

12"

11 **GARDEN WALL SECTION**
Scale   1/2"=1'0"

LIMESTONE CAP

TOP OF PARAPET
EL. 705.75

ROOF SLAB
EL. 703.75

8" CMU (SOLID)

ROOF SLAB

4' FACE BRICK

2/-

1½" AIR SPACE

5 BRICK COURSE PER COIN

FIRST FLOOR
EL. 692.17

LIMESTONE BAND

UPPER LEVEL SLAB

BUILDING SECTION

Fig. 1.7 *Building and Site Sections and Elevations*

8

PERSPECTIVE CONSTRUCTION—THE BASICS

As we observe our surroundings, an object such as a building that is close to us appears to be larger than the same size building that is further away from us. As the distance increases, the objects become smaller and smaller until they disappear from view. (See Figure 1.8)

Consider, next, a row of street trees, a railroad track, or a tall building such as the Sears Tower in Chicago. With each of these there are two parallel lines, either horizontal or vertical, which appear to converge to a single point at our eye level, and then disappear beyond that point. These common everyday experiences are simply the same basics that apply to perspective drawing. (See Figure 1.9)

As we study the basics of perspective construction, we will examine these relationships between the viewer (you) and the object. We will illustrate the results of these relationships on the drawing board, which is a two-dimensional pictorial plane. Before we actually begin practicing perspective construction, it is necessary to understand the perspective terms commonly used. (See Figure 1.10)

The object: It could be a single object or a group, or a row of objects. It can be located at any distance or at any angle in relation to the viewer.

The visual rays (VR): We see an object through visual rays. Two visual rays form a line, and numerous visual rays form the appearance of an object. (See Figure 1.11)

The station point (SP): The station point is the position from which you view the object. Its location is a matter of choice and depends upon the effect that you are trying to achieve when you draw the object. (See Figures 1.12 to 1.14)

The ground plane (GP): The ground plane is the plane on which the object is placed. For eye level perspective construction, it is always five feet below the eye level. This assumes the average persons height of about 5'6" to 6'0". In aerial view perspective construction, the ground plane can be at any level such as fifty feet or a hundred feet below your eye, depending upon the effect you are trying to create. For a worm's eye view perspective construction, the ground plane can be at equal level with the viewer's eye, or even much higher than eye level.

The picture plane (PP): It is the surface on which the perspective image is drawn. It is always 90° to the ground plane and the center of the vision line. The size of the perspective image decreases as the distance between the picture plane and the object increases. (See Figure 1.15)

The horizon line (HL): The horizon line coincides with the eye level in perspective projection. It is a horizontal line drawn at any distance above or below the ground plane, and all heights are measured in relation to this line.

The cone of vision (COV): Most humans with normal vision can clearly view without moving their heads (on flat ground), an area or cone of approximately 60°.

Objects outside of this limit, although they may be seen, are generally distorted. For the purpose of perspective construction cones of 30 to 40° are commonly used. Since the normal viewing angle is constant, increasing the area to be viewed will require that we increase the distance between the object and the viewer. (See Figure 1.16)

The vanishing point (VP): Vanishing points are the points located on the horizon line from which the parallel lines in the same direction converge. In the case of a two-point perspective, there will be two vanishing points. The angle formed by the two projecting lines from the station points must be 90° in the projection method. (See Figure 1.17) The vanishing points are found by drawing lines from the station point parallel to a major side of the object. The point where they intersect with the horizon line is the vanishing point.

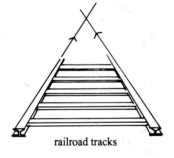
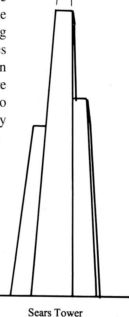

railroad tracks   Sears Tower

Fig. 1.8 *All parallel lines vanish to one point*

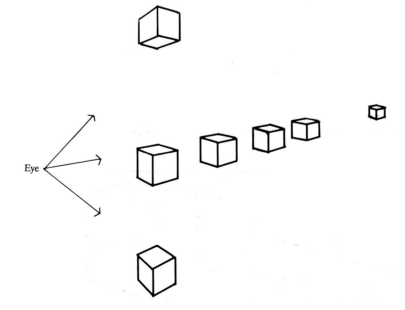

Fig. 1.9 *The perspective of an object varies as the viewing angle varies. A box of equal size appears smaller as the distance from the viewer increases*

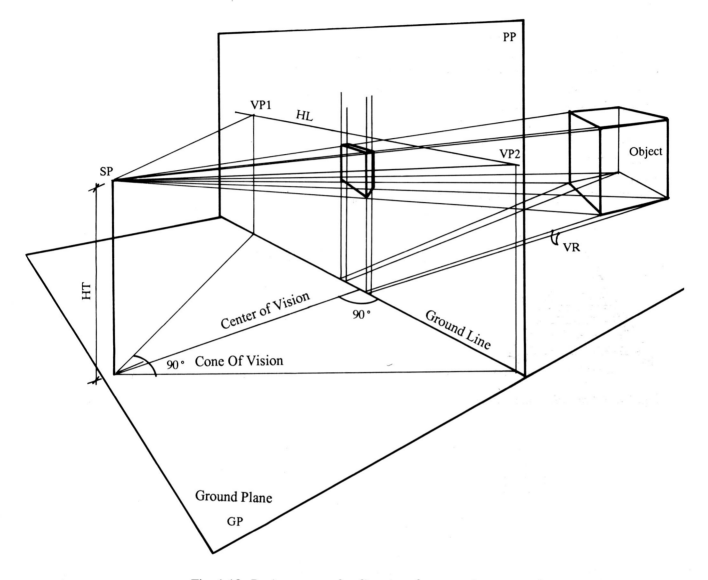

Fig. 1.10 *Basic terms and a diagram of a two-point perspective*

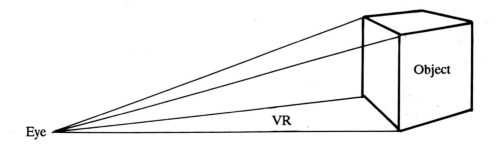

Fig. 1.11 *Numerous rays form the appearance of an object*

11

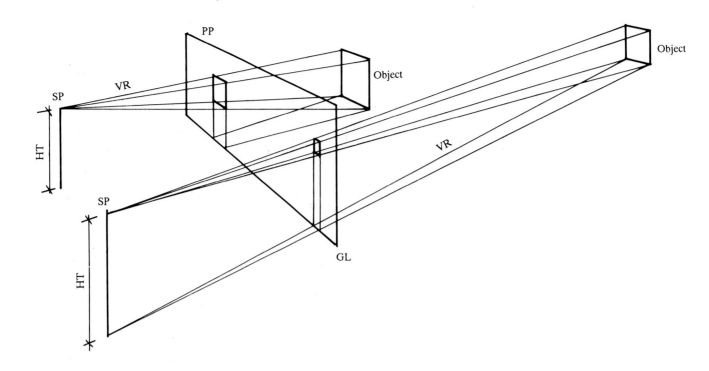

Fig. 1.12 *An object of the same size. Its perspective image reduces as the distance between the station point and the object increases*

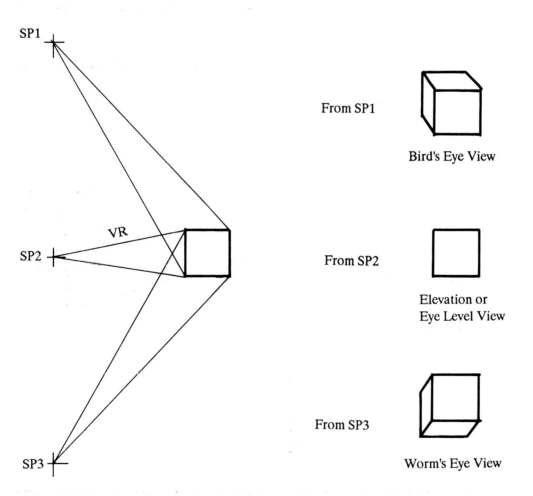

From SP1

Bird's Eye View

From SP2

Elevation or
Eye Level View

From SP3

Worm's Eye View

Fig. 1.13 *The perspective image varies as the station point moves vertically*

12

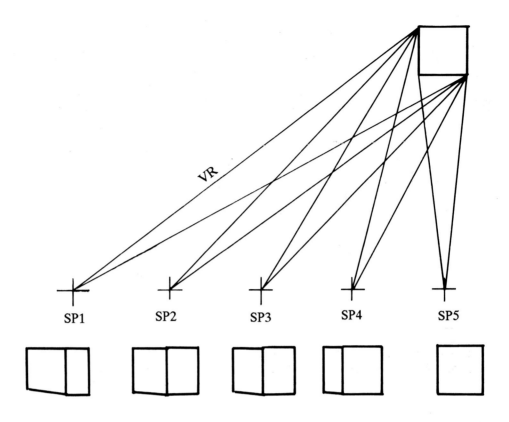

Fig. 1.14 *The perspective image of the cube varies as the station point moves horizontally*

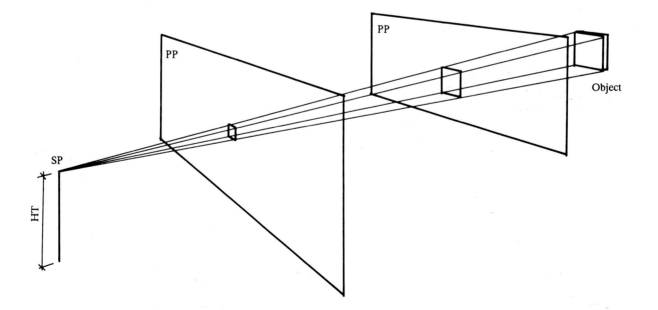

Fig. 1.15 *The perspective image reduces as the distance between the picture plane and the object increases*

13

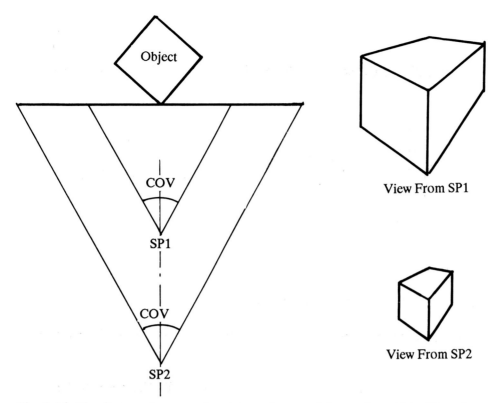

Fig. 1.16 *The distance between the picture plane and the station point affects the size of the object in perspective. To increase the area to be viewed increases the distance between the object and the viewer.*

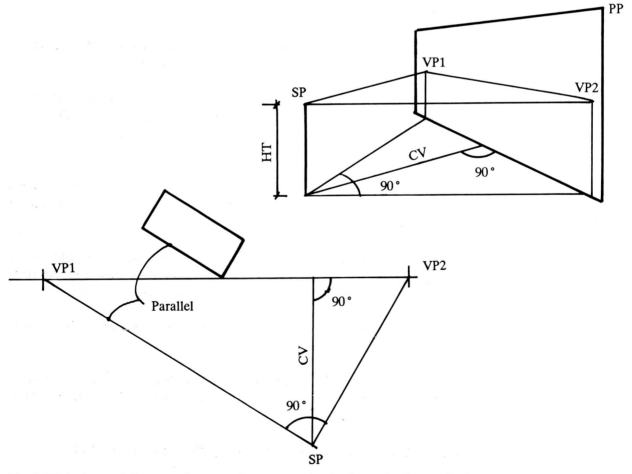

Fig. 1.17 *A plan and diagram of perspective construction by the projection method*

PERSPECTIVE CONSTRUCTION WITH PROJECTION METHOD

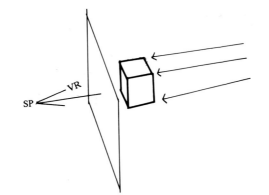

Fig. 1.18 *One-point perspective*

One-Point Perspective of a Room (interior)

Step 1 Draw the plan and elevation of a room to the same scale of 1/8" = 1'0". (See Figure 1.19)

Step 2 Draw the picture plane (PP). In this case the PP coincides with the line of the end wall. (See Figure 1.19)

Step 3 Locate a station point (SP) in front of the plane at about the center of the PP, and at a distance twice the width of the picture plane. Draw the center of the vision (CV) line 90° to the PP. (See Figure 1.19)

Step 4 Check the cone of vision (COV). It should be 60° or less, and the area to be shown in the perspective is within the limit. (See Figure 1.19)

Step 5 Draw the end wall of the room in 1/8" scale above the plan at any distance. Draw the horizon line (HL) 5' above the ground line (GL). Locate the vanishing point (VP). It is the point where the center of the vision line intersects the horizon line. (See Figure 1.20)

Step 6 To locate the furniture draw a one foot grid line on the plan and perspective view. For convenience we enlarge the plan to 1/4 scale. From the VP project the lines. (See Figure 1.20)

Step 7 To locate the furniture in depth, use the dividing method by subdividing the side wall. Carry the lines to the floor where they intersect the projection lines from the PP for the horizontal location of the furniture. (See Figure 1.21)

Step 8 For any furniture placed other than at 90° to the PP, establish additional VPs as required.

Step 9 From the side of the end wall (used as a vertical measuring line), project height of all the furniture to meet the vertical projection from the horizontal locations. (See Figure 1.21)

Step 10 Add details, and complete the perspective. (See Figure 1.22)

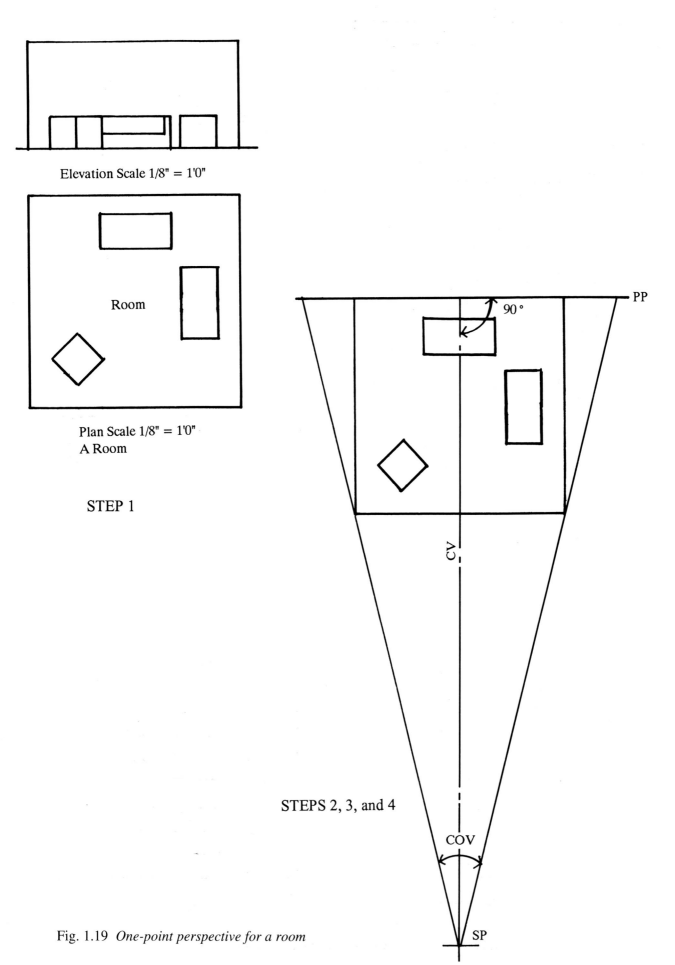

Elevation Scale 1/8" = 1'0"

Room

Plan Scale 1/8" = 1'0"
A Room

STEP 1

90°

PP

CV

STEPS 2, 3, and 4

COV

SP

Fig. 1.19 *One-point perspective for a room*

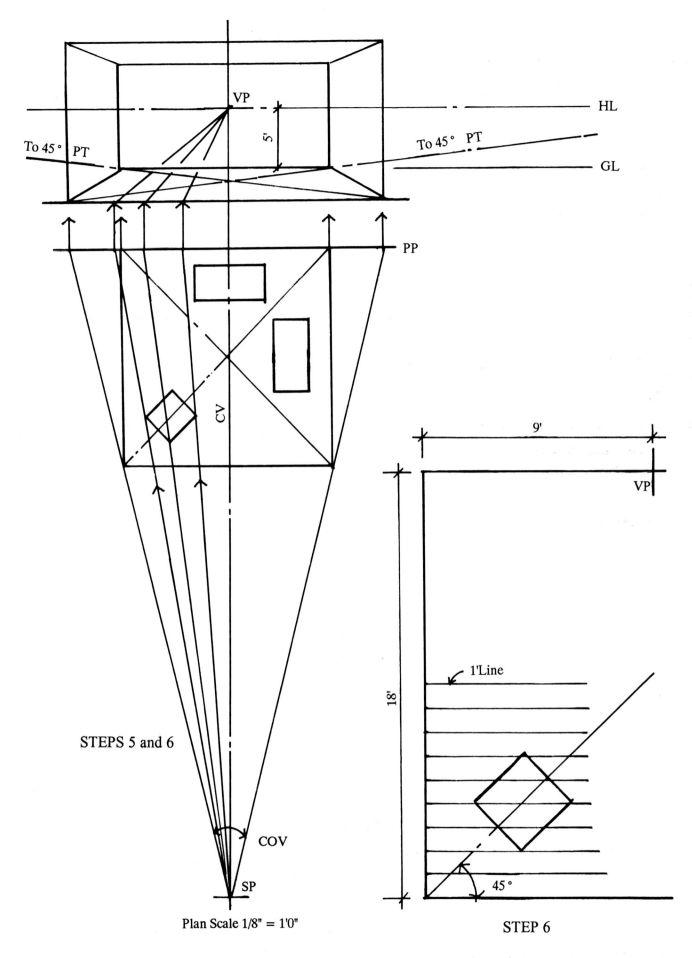

HL

VP

5'

To 45° PT

To 45° PT

GL

PP

CV

STEPS 5 and 6

COV

SP

Plan Scale 1/8" = 1'0"

9'

VP

1'Line

18'

45°

STEP 6

Fig. 1.20 *One-point perspective for a room, see Fig. 1.19*

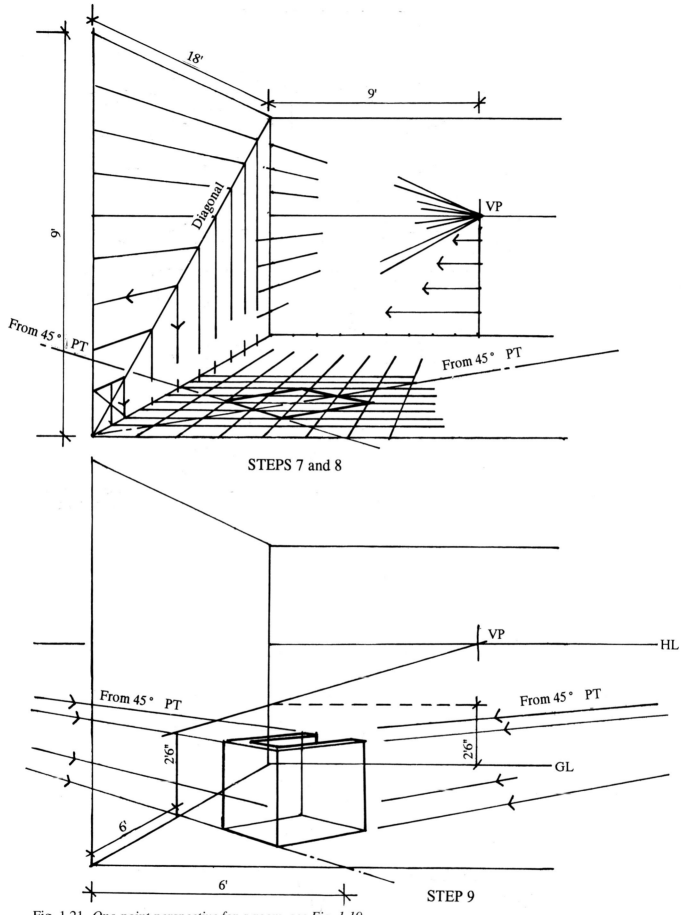

18'

9'

9'

Diagonal

From 45° PT

From 45° PT

VP

STEPS 7 and 8

VP

HL

From 45° PT

From 45° PT

2'6"

2'6"

GL

6'

6'

STEP 9

Fig. 1.21 *One-point perspective for a room, see Fig. 1.19*

18

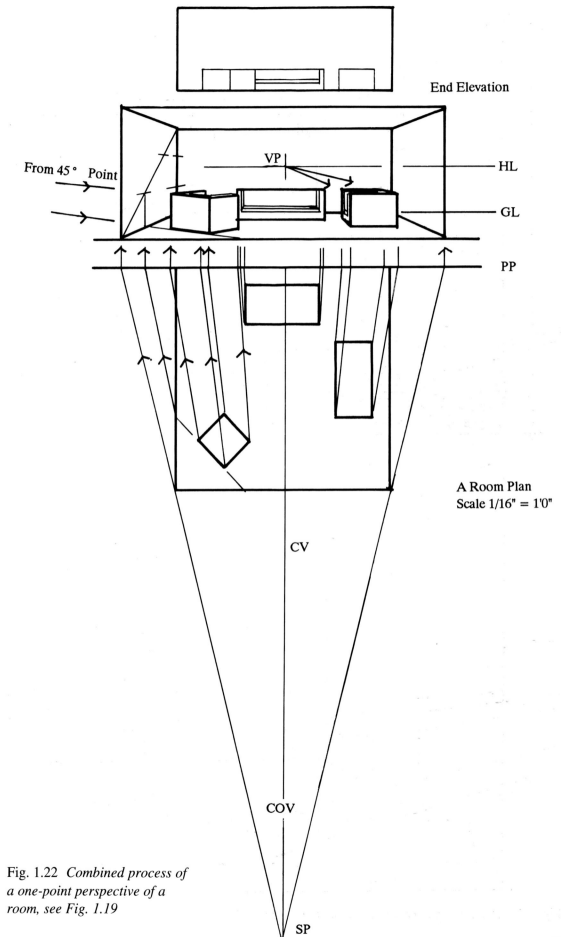

End Elevation

From 45° Point

VP

HL

GL

PP

A Room Plan
Scale 1/16" = 1'0"

CV

COV

SP

Fig. 1.22 *Combined process of
a one-point perspective of a
room, see Fig. 1.19*

19

One-Point Perspective of a garden (exterior)

Step 1 Draw the plan to a scale that is convenient with which to work. Since the scale you select relates directly to the size of the final perspective drawing, you may need to test the best scale to get the size results you want. (See Figure 1.23)

Step 2 Add all dimensions (width and length), and elevations on the plan. (See Figure 1.23)

Step 3 Locate PP. In this case the picture plane (PP) coincides with the end of the garden. (See Figure 1.24)

Step 4 Locate the station point (SP). In this situation, it is located in the room where the view is toward the garden. (See Figure 1.24)

Step 5 Check the cone of vision (COV). It should be 60° or less, and the area to be shown in the perspective is within the limit. The center of the vision line is 90° to the PP. (See Figure 1.24)

Step 6 Draw a ground line (GL) parallel to the picture plane (PP) at any distance. In this case the ground line coincides with the end of the garden. Therefore, the end

(continued on page 23)

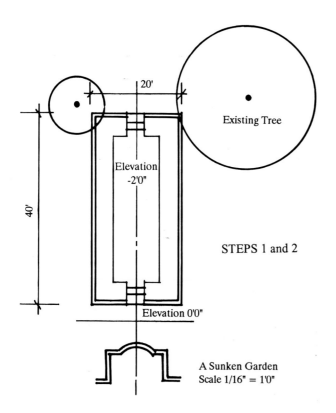

20'

40'

Elevation
-2'0"

Existing Tree

STEPS 1 and 2

Elevation 0'0"

A Sunken Garden
Scale 1/16" = 1'0"

Fig. 1.23 *One-point perspective using measuring points*

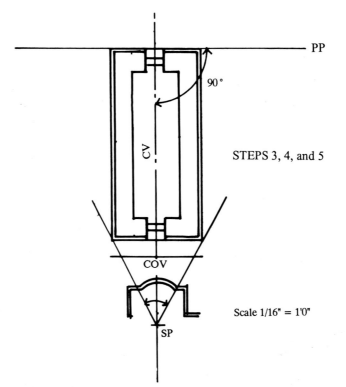

PP

90°

CV

COV

SP

STEPS 3, 4, and 5

Scale 1/16" = 1'0"

Fig. 1.24 *One-point perspective, see Fig. 1.23*

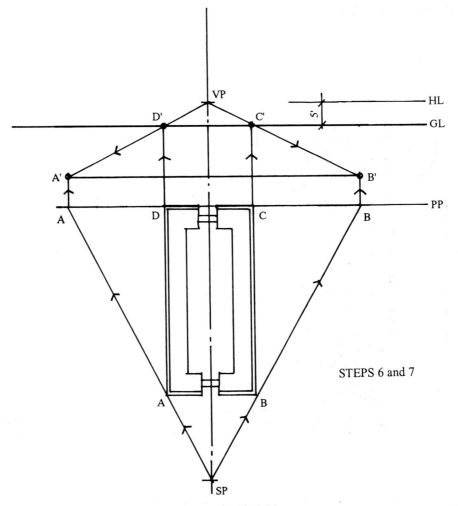

VP

HL

5'

D'   C'   GL

A'   B'

A   D   C   B   PP

A   B

SP

STEPS 6 and 7

Fig. 1.25 *One-point perspective, see Fig. 1.23*

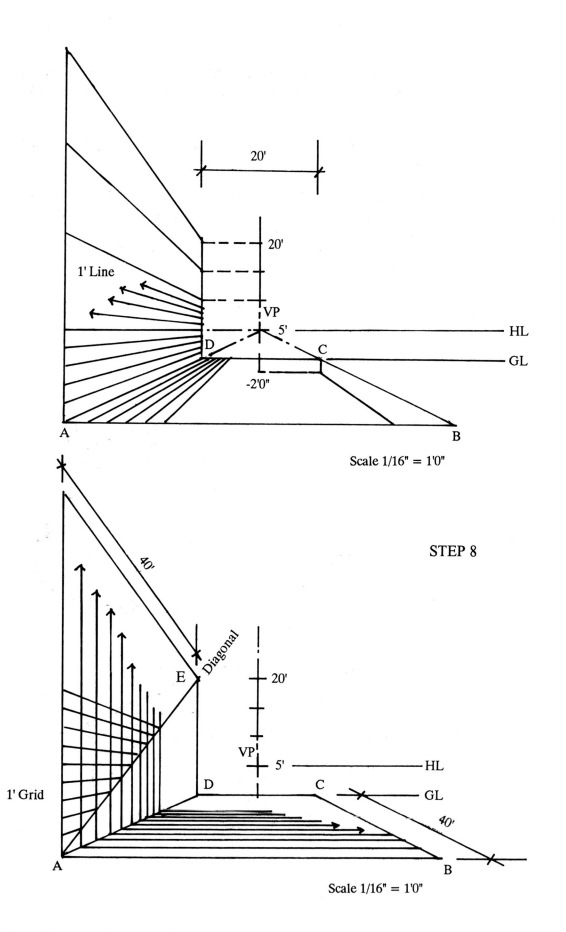

Fig. 1.26 *One-point perspective, see Fig. 1.23*

elevation has the same scale as the plan, CD = C'D'. Locate the vanishing point (VP). It is on the center of the vision (CV) line, and 5 feet above the ground line. (See Figure 1.25)

Step 7 Locate points A, B, A' and B' at the intersection of the lines projected from VP and SP. (See Figure 1.25)

Step 8 From VP plot one foot lines on the side elevation and on the ground plane, at 1/16" scale, as well as for the depressed area. Draw the diagonal line AE either on the side elevation or on the ground plane that intersects the lines projected from VP. Each intersection is one foot apart. Complete the one foot grid. Elements in the plan can be easily located. (See Figure 1.26)

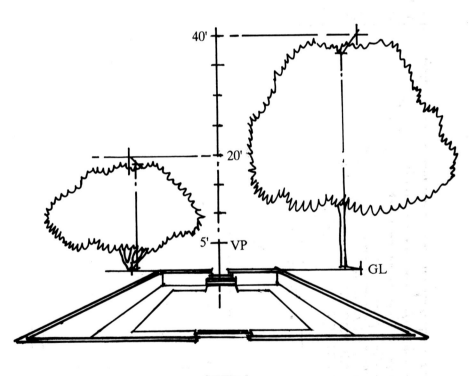

STEP 9

Fig. 1.27 *One-point perspective, see Fig. 1.23*

23

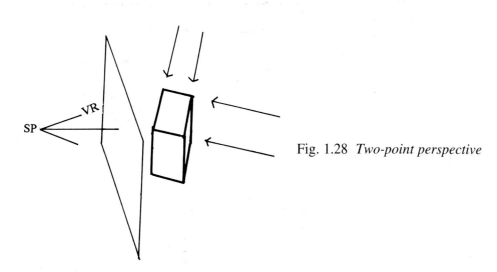

Fig. 1.28 *Two-point perspective*

Step 9 Complete the detail of the garden. (See Figure 1.27)

Two-Point Perspective of a House

Step 1 Draw the plan and elevations at a convenient scale. (See Figure 1.29)

Step 2 Select a station point (SP) that will be the best viewing location for the object. (See Figure 1.29)

Step 3 Check that the area to be shown on the drawing is within the normal 60° cone of vision, or 30-40° as is usually used. (See Figure 1.29)

Step 4 Locate the center of the vision (CV) line approximately at the center of the object. (See Figure 1.29)

Step 5 Draw the picture plane (PP), 90° to the center of the vision line. (See Figure 1.29)

Step 6 From the station point draw parallel lines to the sides of the object; intersect the picture plane (PP) at vanishing points VP1 and VP2. Extend one side of the object to intersect with the PP, as a point for the vertical measurement line. (See Figure 1.29)

Step 7 Draw a horizon line (HL) parallel to the PP at any convenient distance above the PP. Draw a ground line (GL) parallel to the HL, and 20' below for an aerial view perspective. (See Figure 1.30)

Step 8 Project lines from the SP to all corners of the object, and meet the PP at various points. (See Figure 1.30)

Step 9 To locate the base of the object, draw a line from VP1 through the base of the height line. Continue until the line intersects with the vertical projection line of the respective corner. (See Figure 1.30)

Step 10 Complete the remaining lines and details with VP1 and VP2. (See Figure 1.31)

24

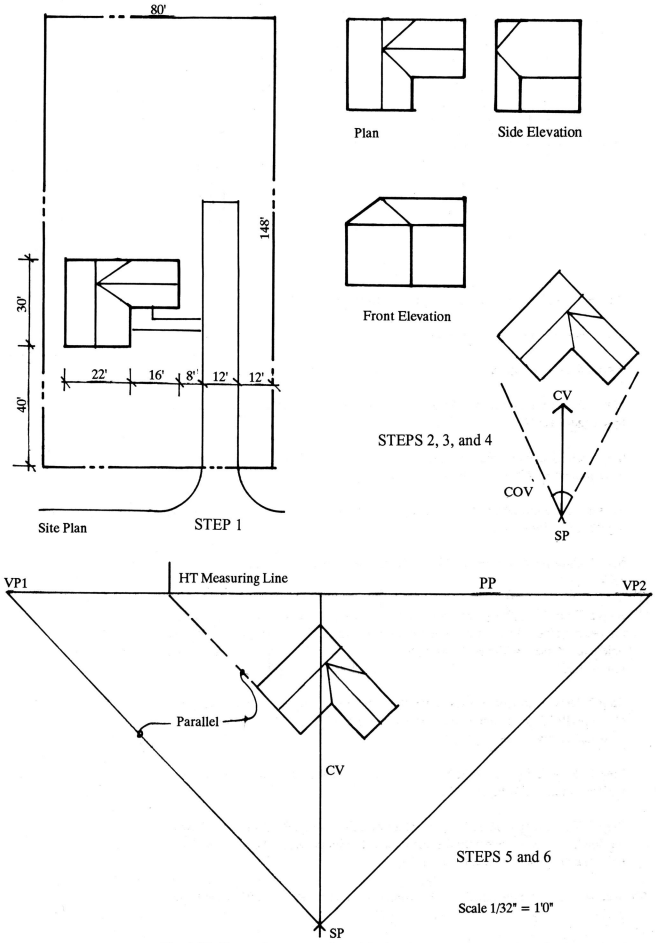

80'

148'

30'

40'

22'   16'   8'   12'   12'

Site Plan   STEP 1

Plan   Side Elevation

Front Elevation

STEPS 2, 3, and 4

CV

COV

SP

VP1   HT Measuring Line   PP   VP2

Parallel

CV

STEPS 5 and 6

Scale 1/32" = 1'0"

SP

Fig. 1.29 *Two-point perspective with visual rays*

25

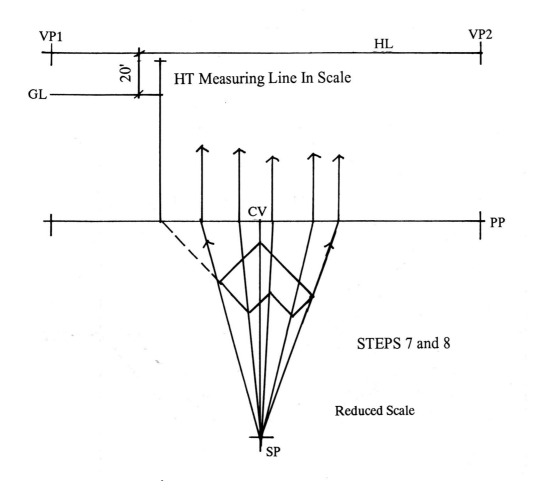

VP1

HL

VP2

20'

GL

HT Measuring Line In Scale

CV

PP

STEPS 7 and 8

Reduced Scale

SP

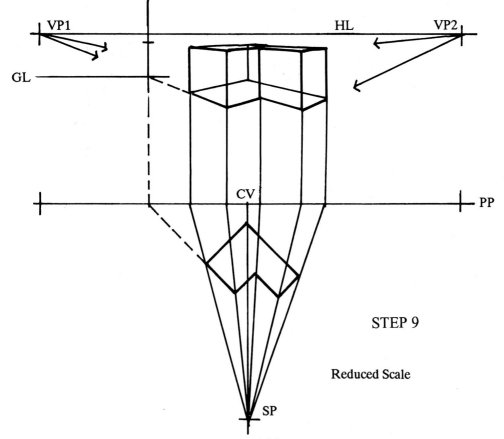

VP1

HL

VP2

GL

CV

PP

STEP 9

Reduced Scale

SP

Fig. 1.30 *Two-point perspective, see Fig. 1.29*

26

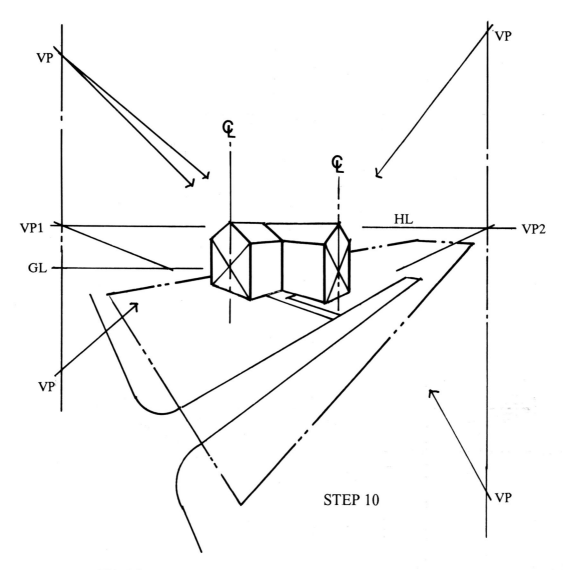

VP

VP

℄

℄

VP1

HL

VP2

GL

VP

STEP 10

VP

Fig. 1.31 *Two-point perspective, see Fig. 1.29*

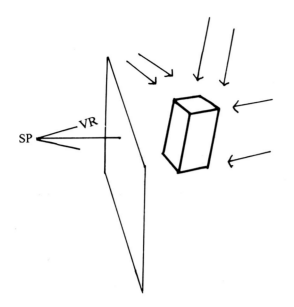

Fig. 1.32 *Three-point perspective*

Three-Point Perspective of a Box

Step 1 The plan of the object is drawn at any angle and any scale. (See Figure 1.33)

Step 2 Draw a side elevation of the object, with incline picture plane (PP). X is the distance between the object and the bottom (BP) of the picture plane (PP). (See Figure 1.33)

Step 3 Locate both station points (SP) in plan and elevation. W is the distance from the object. (See Figure 1.33)

Step 4 Identify vanishing points VP1 and VP2 as you did for two-point perspective construction previously, parallel to line AD and AB. (See Figure 1.33)

Step 5 From the SP in the plan, obtain points of intersection on the top (TP) and bottom (BP) of the picture plane (PP). Project all these points vertically down. (See Figure 1.34)

Step 6 From the SP in elevation, obtain points of intersection on the picture plane. Project all these points horizontally right. (See Figure 1.34)

Step 7 Where two lines meet, A'B'C'D' are located. Locate A"B"C"D" by the same method. (See Figure 1.34)

Step 8 Connect B'B" and the third vanishing point is located. (See Figure 1.34)

Step 9 Complete the object with lines from VP1, VP2 and VP3. This connects A' to D', B' to A' and so forth. (See Figure 1.36)

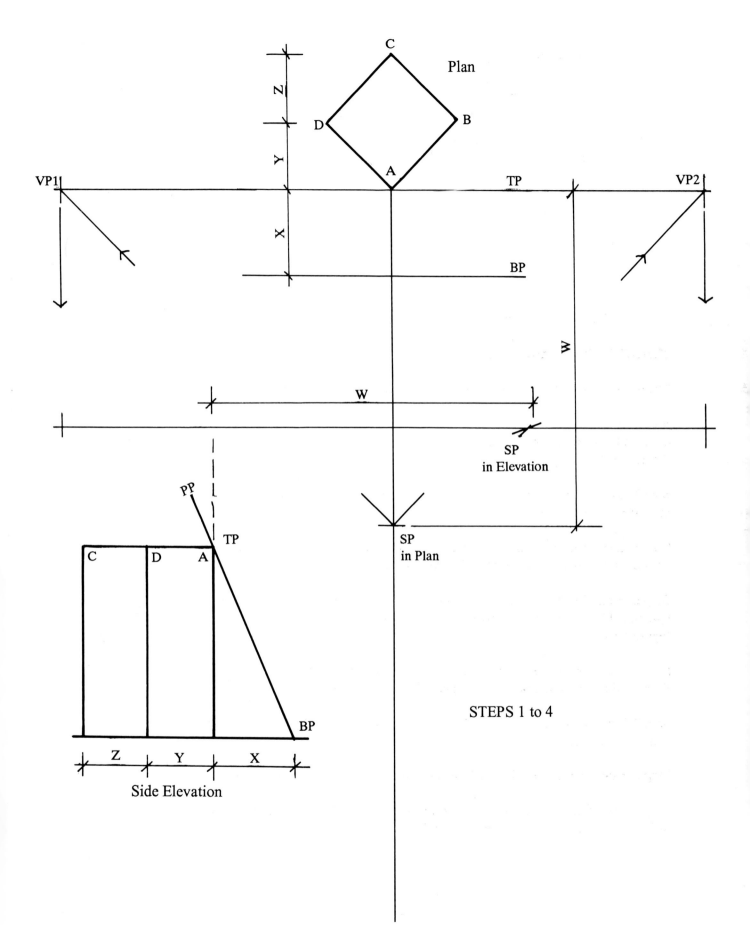

Fig. 1.33 *Three-point perspective by visual rays projection*

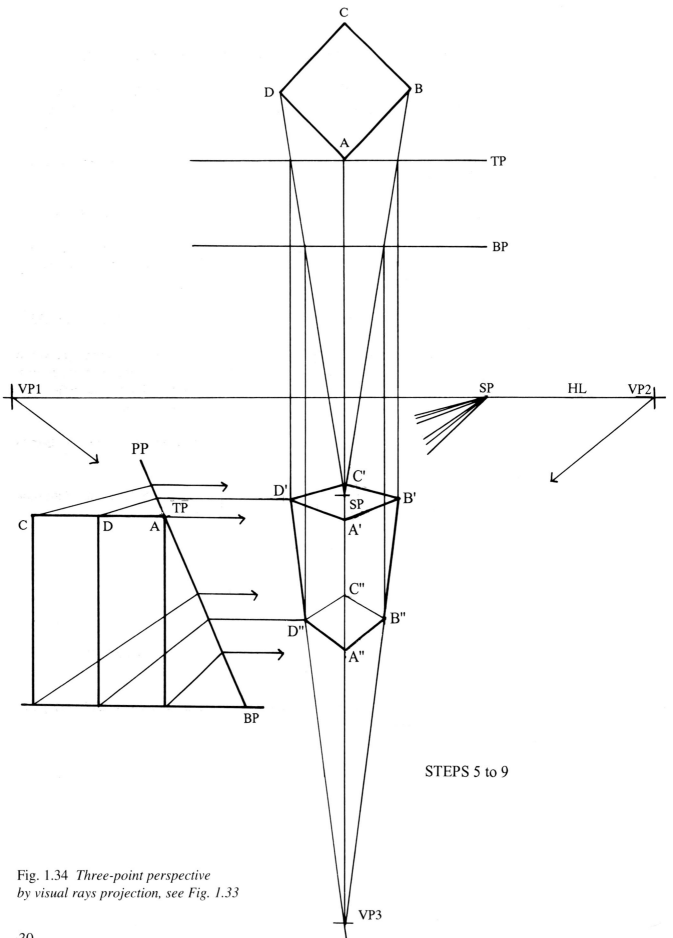

STEPS 5 to 9

Fig. 1.34 *Three-point perspective*
by visual rays projection, see Fig. 1.33

ALTERNATIVE METHOD OF PERSPECTIVE CONSTRUCTION

An alternative method for constructing a perspective without using projection method is to locate measuring points for depth and width. From these you can complete the object in perspective.

One-Point Perspective of a Garden (See Figure 1.18 for an illustration of a one-point perspective.)

Step 1 Draw plan to scale and mark all elevation changes, if any. (See Figure 1.35)

Step 2 Draw a horizontal line (HL). The distance from the ground line is optional. In this case HL is 22'6" above the ground line. Locate 45° point (PT), approximately three times the length of the object. (See Figure 1.35)

Step 3 Draw a width line parallel to the HL, at any distance. (See Figure 1.35)

Step 4 Project from VP, object width of the garden (20'). Draw depth line 90° to the width line from the VP. Since all diagonal lines of a square are parallel, they converge to one point. To obtain the depth of the garden, simply project from 45° PT the depth of the garden (40') thus laid out. (See Figure 1.36)

Step 5 Complete details by applying the grid on the plan and transferring them to perspective view.

Step 6 Adjust distance between HL and width line (equal to GL) and VP location to obtain various viewing heights and viewing angles.

Two-Point Perspective of a Box 30°/45° (Figure 1.37)

Two-Point Perspective of a Box 30°/60° (Figure 1.38)

Two-Point Perspective of an Aerial View of a House (Figure 1.39)

Two and Three-Point Aerial Perspective View of a High Rise Building (Figures 1.40 and 1.41)

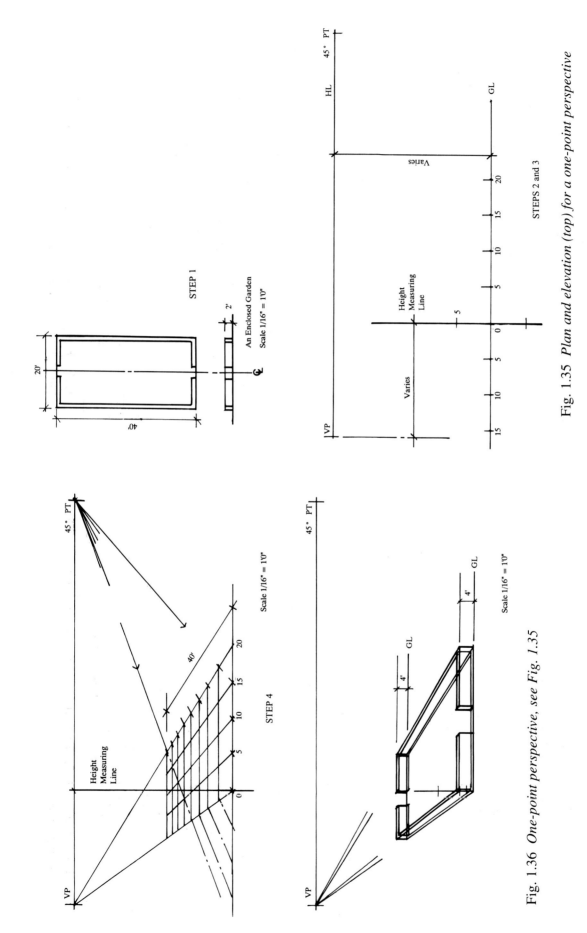

Fig. 1.35 *Plan and elevation (top) for a one-point perspective*

Fig. 1.36 *One-point perspective, see Fig. 1.35*

32

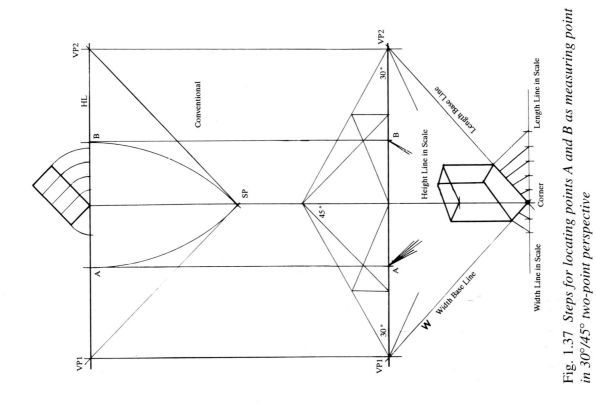

Fig. 1.37 Steps for locating points A and B as measuring point in 30°/45° two-point perspective

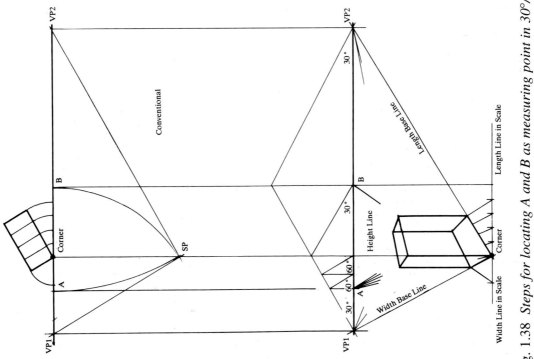

Fig. 1.38 Steps for locating A and B as measuring point in 30°/60° two-point perspective

33

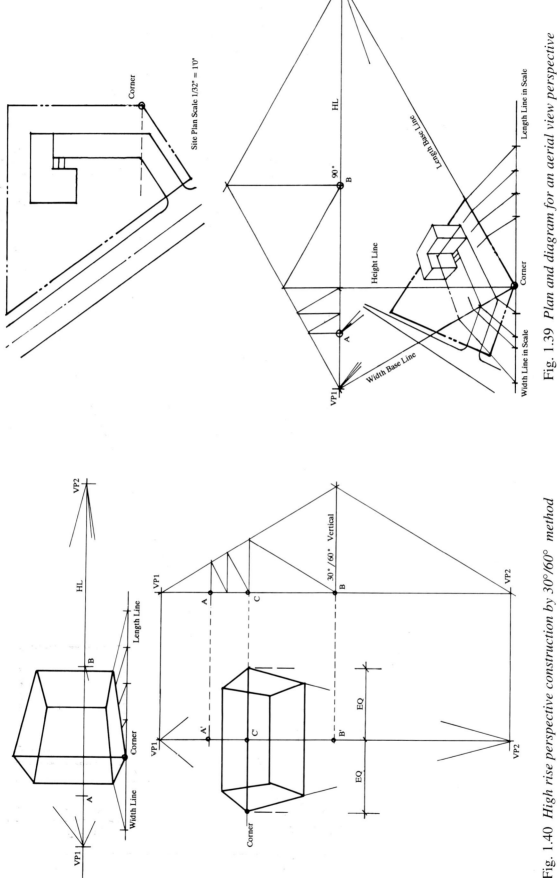

Site Plan Scale 1/32" = 10'

Fig. 1.39 *Plan and diagram for an aerial view perspective*

Fig. 1.40 *High rise perspective construction by 30°/60° method (top). Bird's eye view construction using 30°/60° method (bottom)*

34

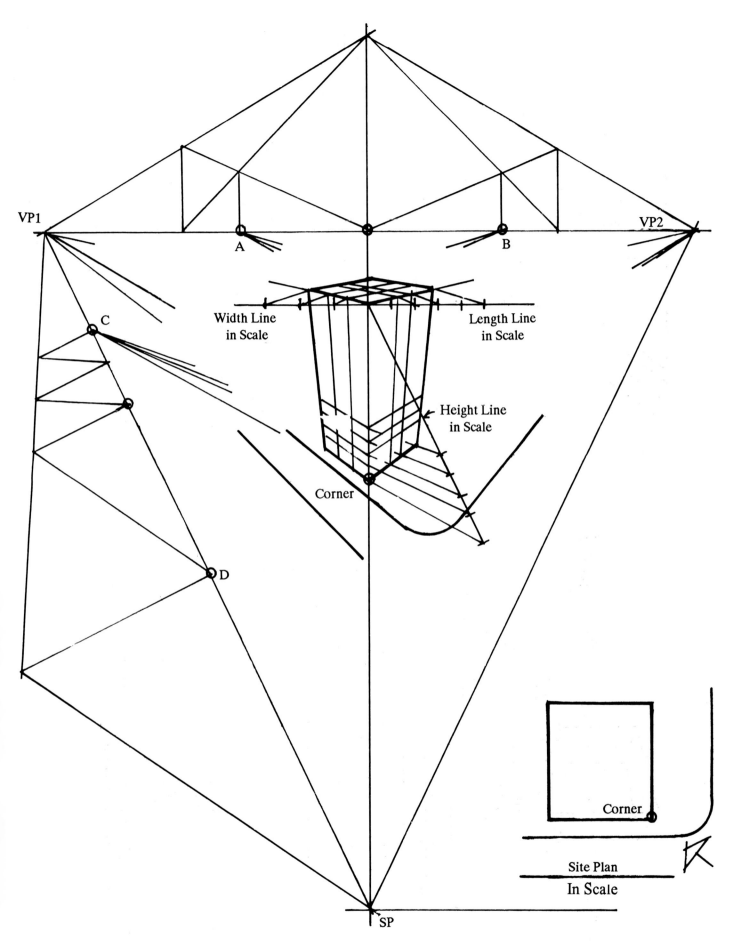

Fig. 1.41 *Three-point perspective aerial view of a high rise*

PERSPECTIVE CHART METHOD

There are many perspective charts and grids available on the market. Perspective construction is no longer a time consuming work. A roughout can be done in a couple of hours, compared with considerable hours by the projection method. In order to utilize the chart effectively, one should have the basic knowledge of perspective theory.

Charts of 30°, 45°, and 60° projection, eye level and aerial views can be used singly or combined. These can be the multi-grid series or the Perspective Charts by Lawson, either of which can be purchased commercially at any art supply stores. A typical perspective chart by P. Lawson appears on page 37, Figure 1.42. (Reprinted from PERPSECTIVE CHARTS by permission of the Publisher, Van Nostrand Reinhold, all rights reserved.)

The horizon line (HL), vanishing points (VP), and vertical measuring line are indicated on the charts. Projection lines are broken down into unit grids that can be converted into any scale. The finished product is accurate and can be most useful.

Step 1 Select view point (SP).

Step 2 Determine scale.

Step 3 Draw 10' grids on the site plan, and check the area to be shown and be sure it is within the final drawing size. You also can reduce the finished rough after construction.

Step 4 Plot the ground plane (GP) on the chart.

Step 5 Transfer all vertical measurements by projection from the vertical measuring line along the base line.

Step 6 Add details and complete the perspective.

(See Figures 1.43 to 1.48)

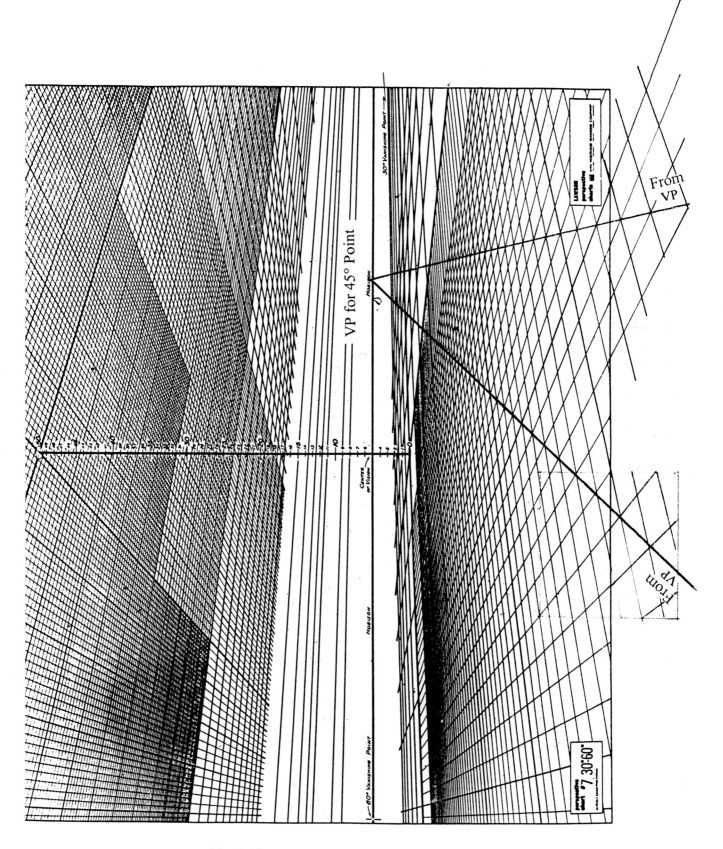

Fig. 1.42 *A typical perspective chart by Lawson. To draw a larger image means to locate the object closer to you on the chart. To extend the chart, find 45° point on the Horizon and use the same to VPs to extend the grid.*

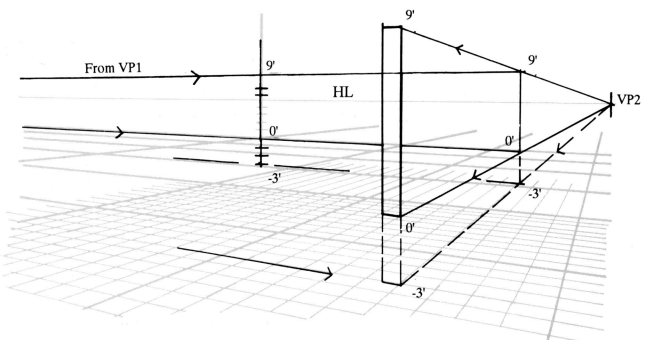

Fig. 1.43 *Eye level perspective construction using chart method*

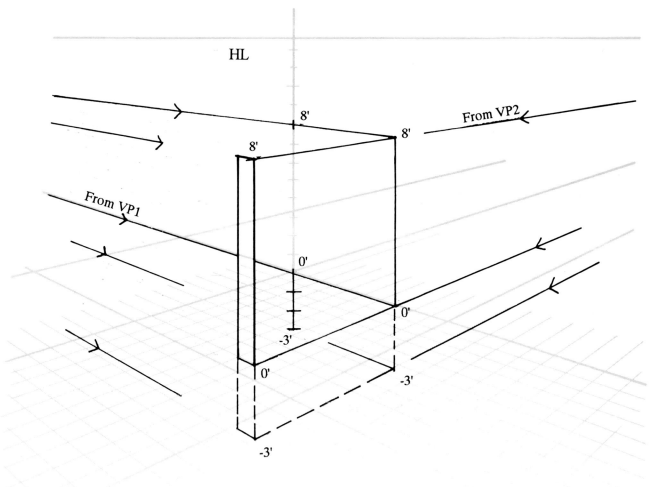

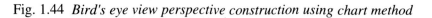

Fig. 1.44 *Bird's eye view perspective construction using chart method*

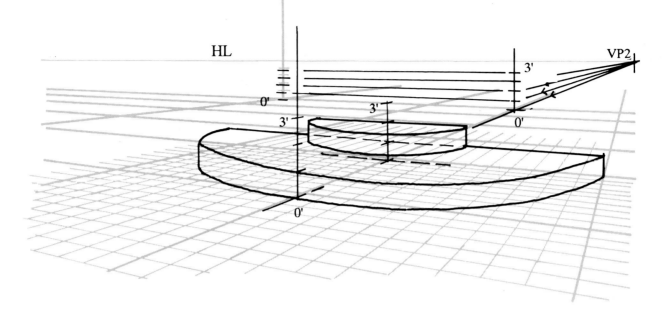

Fig. 1.45 *Perspective of half circles constructed with chart method*

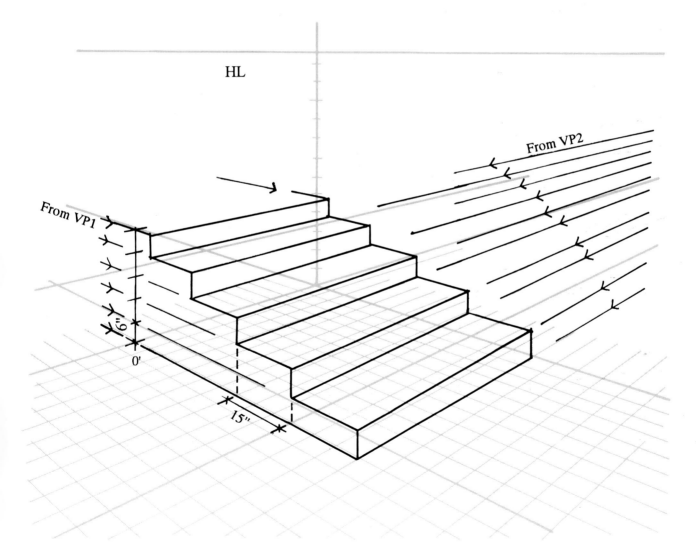

Fig. 1.46 *Perspective of steps constructed with chart method*

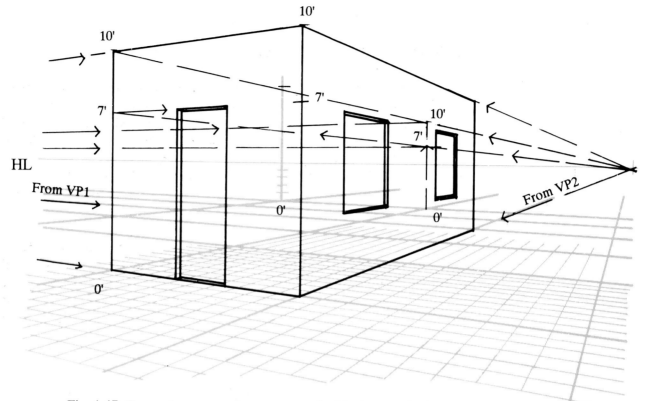

Fig. 1.47 *Two-point perspective constructed with chart method*

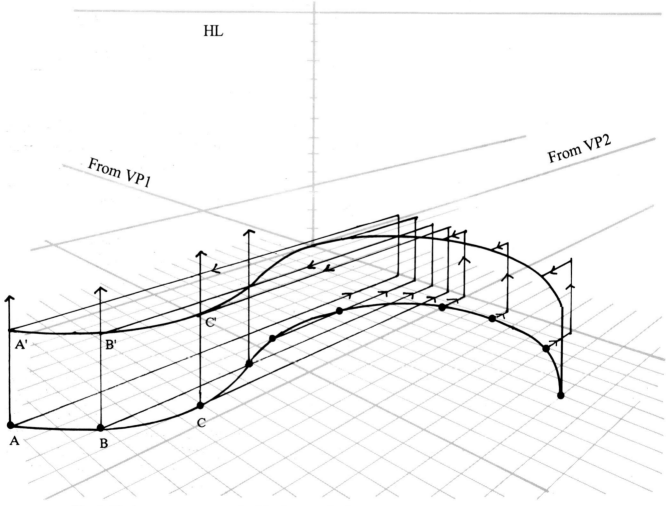

Fig. 1.48 *A curve constructed with chart method*

40

AXONOMETRIC PROJECTION

This is a method for drawing an object such that the height, width, and depth dimensions are shown in their actual scale measurements, or by a chosen ratio. Height is plotted at 90° to the plan vertically, while depth and width are projected from a chosen angle. The simplest axonometric perpendicular projection is isometric projection. Its depth:width:height (D:W:H) ratio is 1:1:1. Commonly used angle combinations are 45°-45°, 30°-60°, 30°-30°, and angle a: 90°-a. [Angle means direction of projection. For example, if we use angle a=50° (D), then 90°-50°=40° (W).]

Its appearance is very much distorted. Other commonly used ratios of D:W:H are 1/2:1:1, 1/3:1:1, and 1/2:1:1. The advantage of this method is that the drawing will show an overall view; its technique is simple to follow; and the final drawing size can be determined easily. The drawback to this method is that some laypeople (or clients) may have trouble reading or understanding the drawing. (See Figures 1.49 to 1.51)

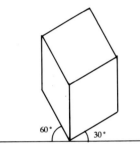

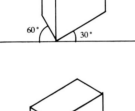

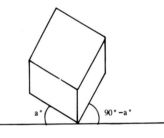

D;W;H 1;1;1/2

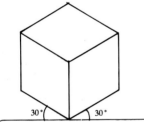

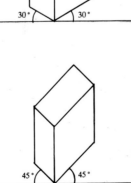

Fig. 1.50 *This is one of the methods used often. The entire picture can be shown on plan with some distortion. All heights are indicated in the same direction at half scale.*

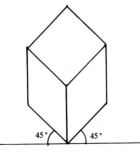

D;W;H 1;1;1

D;W;H 1/2;1;1

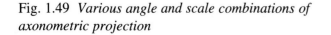

D;W;H 1/2;1;1

Fig. 1.49 *Various angle and scale combinations of axonometric projection*

Fig. 1.51 *The direction of projection is the depth line of the object plotted along a line of 45° incline at either full or half scale of width and height. The appearance of the finished product is badly distorted. The use of this method is limited.*

PERSPECTIVES CONSTRUCTED USING A CAMERA

A bird's eye view can be constructed by using a camera. The perspective produced by this method will not be very accurate. The advantage of this method is that it requires less time, and is very useful when a project does not have enough time or budget available. This technique does not require the knowledge of constructing a perspective. It is a good choice for illustrating a large scale site. Unlike axonometric drawing, it is rather realistic and not distorted.

Lay the site plan flat upon a table. The camera distance to the plan should be far enough so that it will create a receding effect. (See Figure 1.54) The angle of the camera can vary depending upon your choice of view.

The next step is to shoot a slide of the site plan and project it on the wall for tracing. Using full scale or half scale, project the heights of all the elements, and then add the details. A quick and effective bird's eye perspective is completed. A variation of the above method would be directly projecting the vertical height from a site plan. Since the final drawing size will be the same as the site plan, scale can be determined at the beginning.

PERSPECTIVES CONSTRUCTED USING A MODEL (page 44)

When a model is available, a freehand aerial or eye-level perspective roughout can be created in a very short time. Place the model board at any angle on a desk or under a glass-top table (see Figure 1.55). Place a sheet of plexiglass at any angle to the model board. The plexiglass or glass-top serves as a PP. Now, hold the station point (or viewing point) steady, and trace the image directly onto the plexiglass or glass-top (see Figure 1.56 for examples). The view angle can vary as desired. An eye-level view of this method will require a larger model and the placement of the model board will be almost 90 degrees to the glass surface.

42

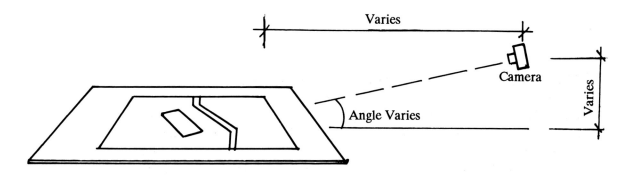

Varies

Camera

Angle Varies

Varies

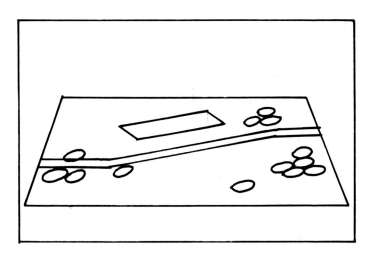

Project slide on wall
and trace the plan

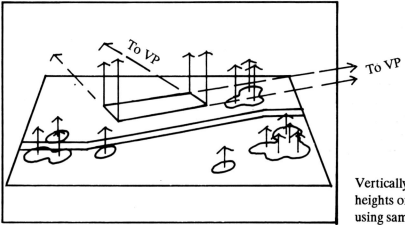

To VP

To VP

Vertically project all
heights of the elements
using same scale

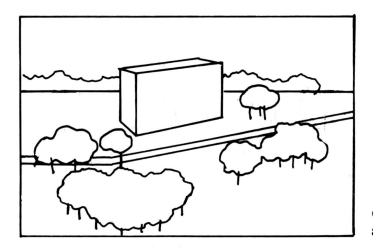

Complete with detail
and finish the drawing

Fig. 1.54 *Bird's eye view perspective constructed by using a camera*

43

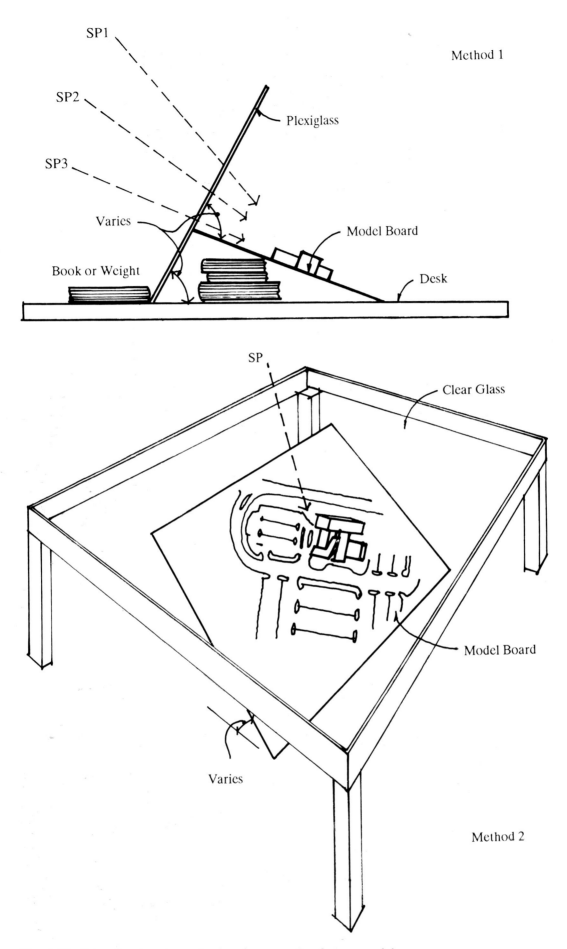

SP1

SP2

SP3

Method 1

Plexiglass

Varies

Model Board

Book or Weight

Desk

SP

Clear Glass

Model Board

Varies

Method 2

Fig. 1.55 *Setup for drawing a freehand perspective from a model*

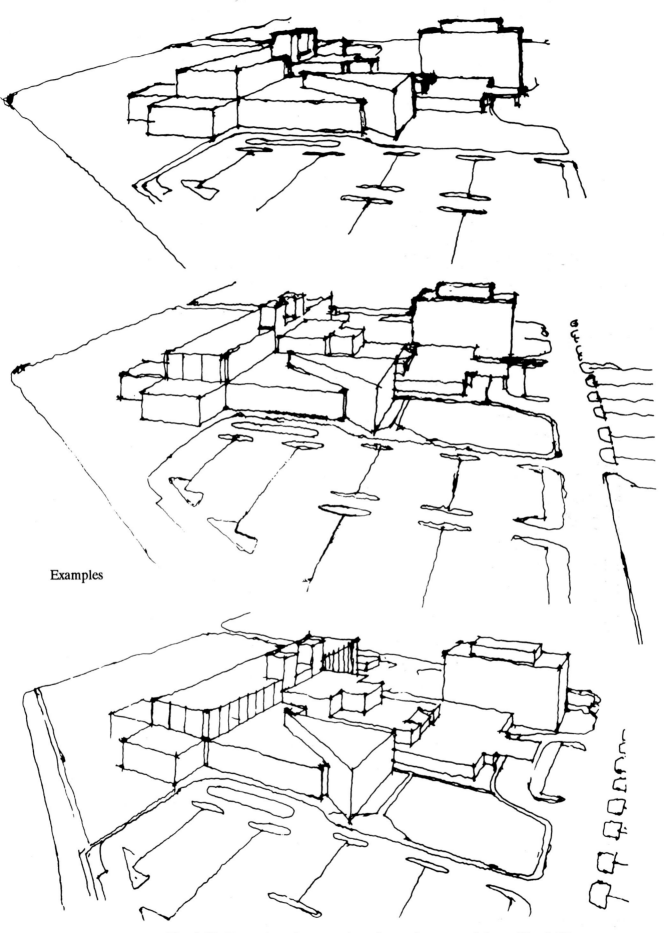

Examples

Fig. 1.56 *Examples of perspectives drawn from a model, see Fig. 1.55*

CONSTRUCTING MISCELLANEOUS ITEMS

Division

The plan and elevation of a rectangle of any size can be divided into equal portions by the center of the two diagonals (see Figures 1.57 to 1.59). There may be times when you need to construct perspectives without any tools such as the charts described earlier. With a basic knowledge of perspectives you can set up a space grid. For example, set up a 10 foot grid. See Figure 1.60. A-A" equals 10 feet. Divide it into two equal parts, A-A' and A'-A". Set the first A-B in depth by visual judgment connecting A-B' and project a line to meet the A"-VP line at C". Carry C" perpendicularly down and intersect A-VP at C. An equal 10 foot grid in depth (B"C"CB) is formed. See Figures 1.60 to 1.62 to use the same method for a horizontal plan.

There are other ways to divide a given length of a line or plane into any number of equal spaces or proportions. The first step is to subdivide the end vertical or horizontal into any proportions that you need. Next, draw a diagonal line from the base of the vertical to the top of the opposite end, and project from the vanishing point to the subdivided points on the vertical line. The exact proportions are then obtained vertically at the point of intersection with the diagonal line. (See Figure 1.63.) The same method applies to the overhead plane and the ground plane. (See Figure 1.64) The third method for (See Figure 1.65) dividing a plane or a line into proportions is to draw a line CA from the end point, any direction from C, divide the line into exact proportions in any scale. Connect A and B, and extend AB to meet the horizon line. From this vanishing point project lines to points C1 to C8 and etc. The same divisions are then transferred to the ground line CB. The proportion of any measurements can be first plotted on CA and transferred to ground line CB. (See Figure 1.66)

Perspective Construction of Steps

The construction of steps follows the same basic rules as applies to other perspectives. The ground line and horizon line are set based upon whether the steps are going up or going down. For a one-point perspective in constructing steps, see Figures 1.67 and 1.68. To construct a two-point perspective for steps, see Figure 1.69.

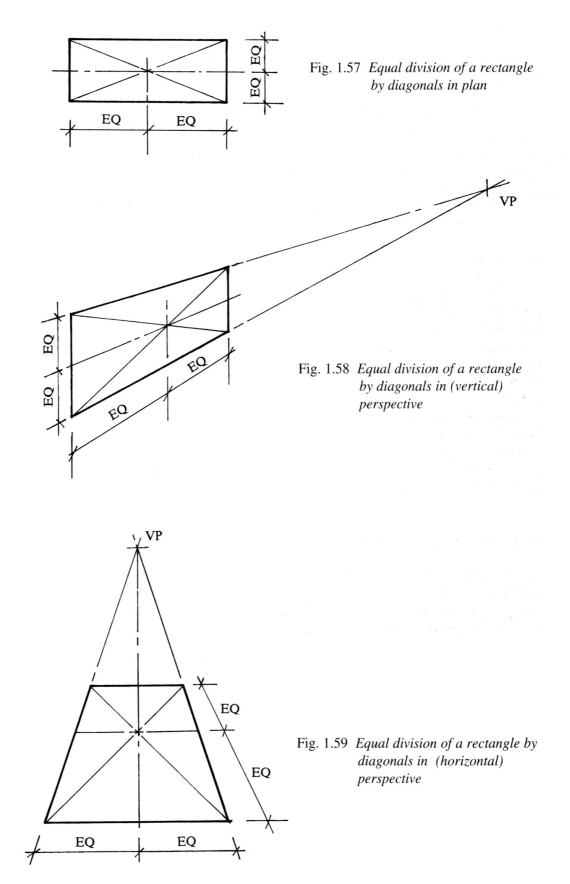

Fig. 1.57 *Equal division of a rectangle by diagonals in plan*

Fig. 1.58 *Equal division of a rectangle by diagonals in (vertical) perspective*

Fig. 1.59 *Equal division of a rectangle by diagonals in (horizontal) perspective*

47

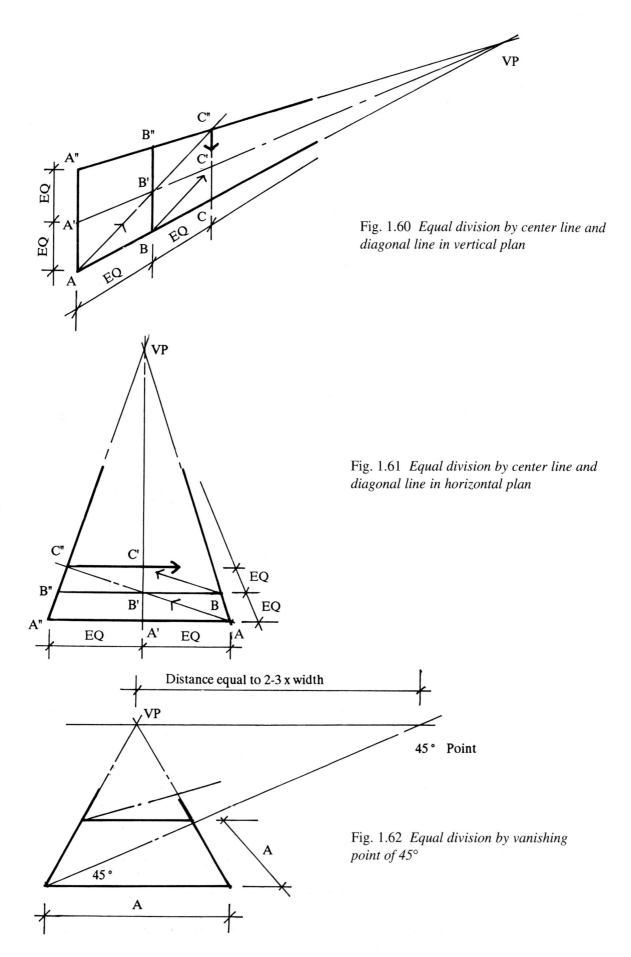

Fig. 1.60 *Equal division by center line and diagonal line in vertical plan*

Fig. 1.61 *Equal division by center line and diagonal line in horizontal plan*

Fig. 1.62 *Equal division by vanishing point of 45°*

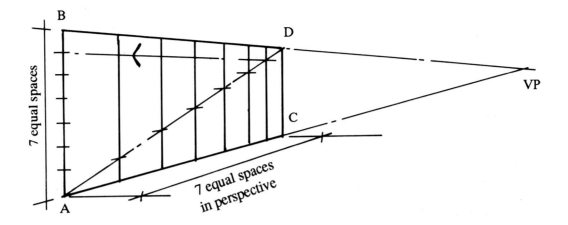

Fig. 1.63 *Division construction by diagonal and vertical measurement lines*

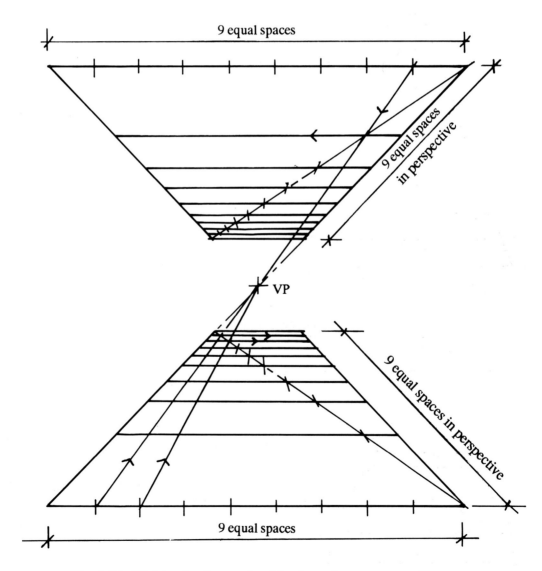

Fig. 1.64 *Division by diagonal and horizontal measurement lines of overhead plane and ground plane*

49

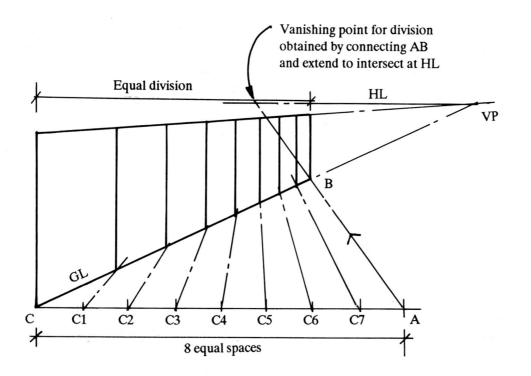

Vanishing point for division
obtained by connecting AB
and extend to intersect at HL

Equal division

HL

VP

B

GL

C   C1   C2   C3   C4   C5   C6   C7   A

8 equal spaces

Fig. 1.65 *Division method 3*

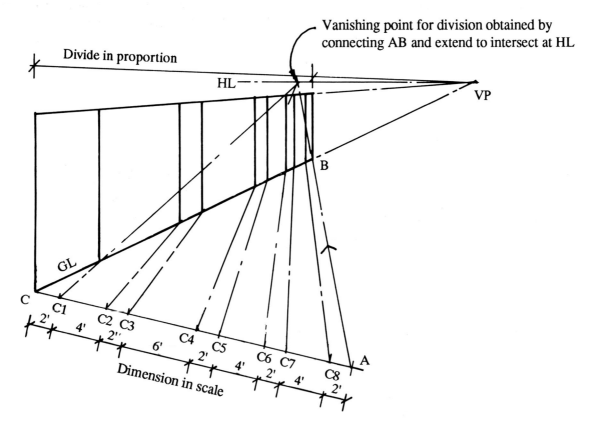

Vanishing point for division obtained by
connecting AB and extend to intersect at HL

Divide in proportion

HL

VP

B

GL

C   C1   C2   C3   C4   C5   C6   C7   C8   A

2'   4'   2"   6'   2'   4'   2'   4'   2'

Dimension in scale

Fig. 1.66 *Division method 3*

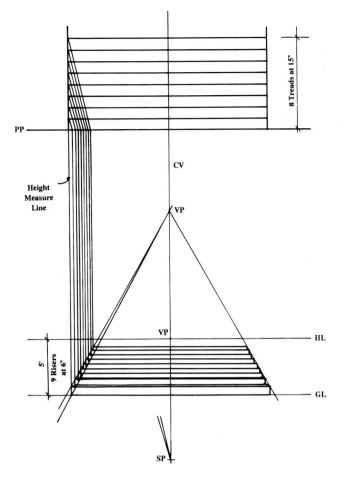

Fig. 1.67 *One-point perspective of steps (rising or going up) by projection method*

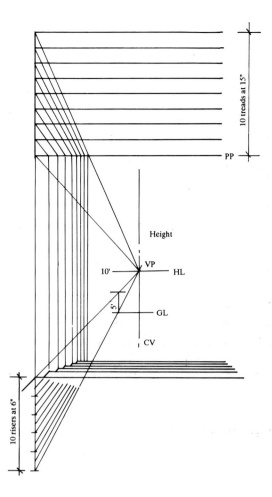

Fig. 1.68 *One-point perspective of steps (down and away from viewer) by projection method*

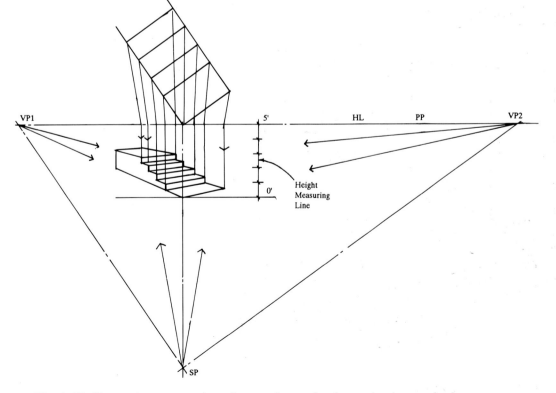

Fig. 1.69 *Two-point perspective of a set of steps by the projection method*

51

Perspective Construction of Circles (Figures 1.70 and 1.71)

Method 1. Divide the square into four equal parts in both directions. Draw diagonals from all four outer rectangles to locate 12 points. Then connect the 12 points to form a circle.

Method 2. Divide 4 equal parts of any side of a square. Form a small square by using one equal part as the length of the side. Draw a diagonal (a) of the small square. Locate a length between the diagonal lines of the large square to obtain the additional point. Repeat the process to locate the other three points. Together with the four mid-points, connect the total of 8 points to form a circle.

Method 3. Draw the two diagonals of a square. Locate point B approximately 1/4 to 1/3 of the length of AC. Repeat four sides. Together with the four mid-points, connect the total of 8 points to form a circle.

Examples of More Than Two Vanishing Points on Same Horizon Line.

When objects are placed randomly on a ground plane, each angle created will require a vanishing point. Since the objects are on the same plane the vanishing point will appear on the same horizon line. (See Figure 1.72)

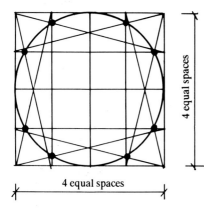

4 equal spaces

METHOD 1

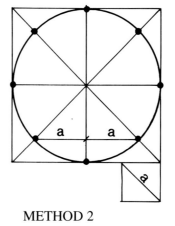

METHOD 2

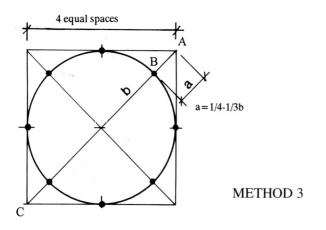

a=1/4-1/3b

METHOD 3

Fig. 1.70 *Three methods for constructing circles in plan*

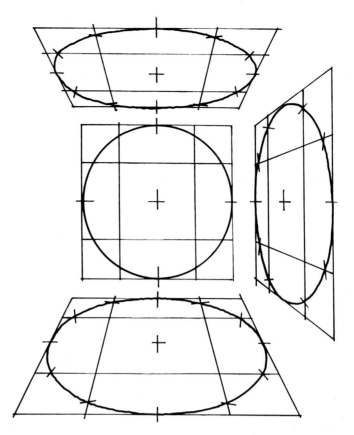

Fig. 1.71 *Perspective view construction of circles in horizontal and vertical planes*

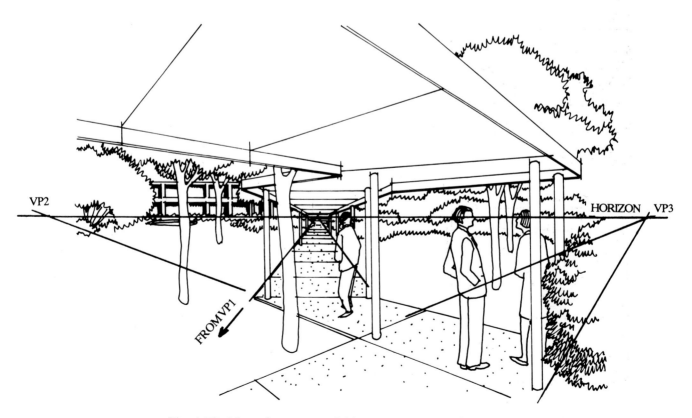

Fig. 1.72 *More than two vanishing points are required to construct the various angles created.*

SPECIAL EFFECTS

Perspectives of Shadows

Shadows in perspective drawing not only give three dimensional effects to the illustrations, but they also add to the overall composition of the picture. In addition, they draw the viewer's attention, suggest the form of the object as well as the surfaces on which the shadows are cast. It would be advantageous to plan at the beginning of the rough sketch and consider shadows as part of the overall composition. For instance, the focal point of the perspective should not be in a shaded area, but instead, the area should have a strong contrast of color and light in order to draw attention.

For exterior and interior perspectives during daylight, the direction of the sun rotates from East to South and West. As for a night scene of interiors, the light source can be multiple; therefore, a diffused light condition is created. Shadows are weaker and softer, edges are less defined. It creates a gradation of shade that in most cases is impossible to imitate. In reality, we have to simplify the construction of the shadow, because it would be too complicated to draw.

In general there are two kinds of light sources. Sun rays originate from an infinite distance. Therefore, they are assumed to be parallel and eventually recede to one vanishing point. Artificial light is regarded as point source. It is from a known distant point and it radiates from that source. The shape of the shadows created by the two kinds of light sources, therefore, are different. (See Figures 1.73 and 1.74)

To construct the shape of a shadow in perspective, we must locate two points: (1.) The vanishing point of the light source (SO); it is determined either arbitrarily or specified by an exact angle, and (2.) The vanishing point of the shadow (SH) on the ground plane that is cast by vertical image of the object. (See Figure 1.75)

Under sunlight, SH is located on the horizon line. For artificial light sources, SH is located on the ground plane. In both cases, SH is in line with the SO and the line SH - SO, is perpendicular to the horizon line and ground plane. (See Figures 1.76 and 1.77)

There are four basic directions of light commonly used in the perspective construction of shadows. The light source may be in front of the station point, from behind the station point, or parallel to the picture plane, either left or right of the object.

Figures 1.78 to 1.100 show various conditions of shadow casting.

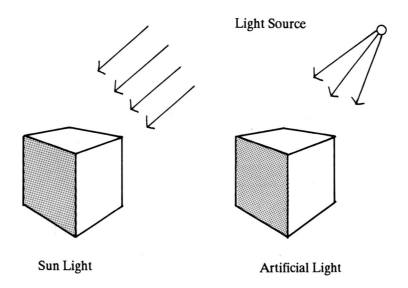

Light Source

Sun Light

Artificial Light

Fig. 1.73 *Two different light sources*

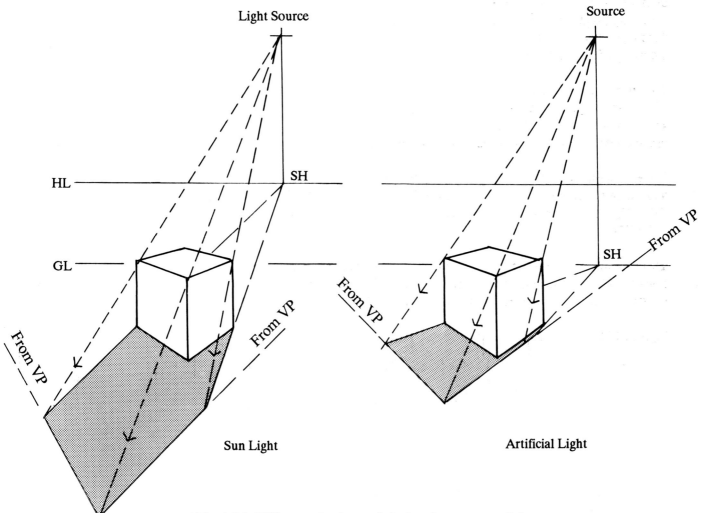

Fig. 1.74 *Difference in shape of shadow between two light sources*

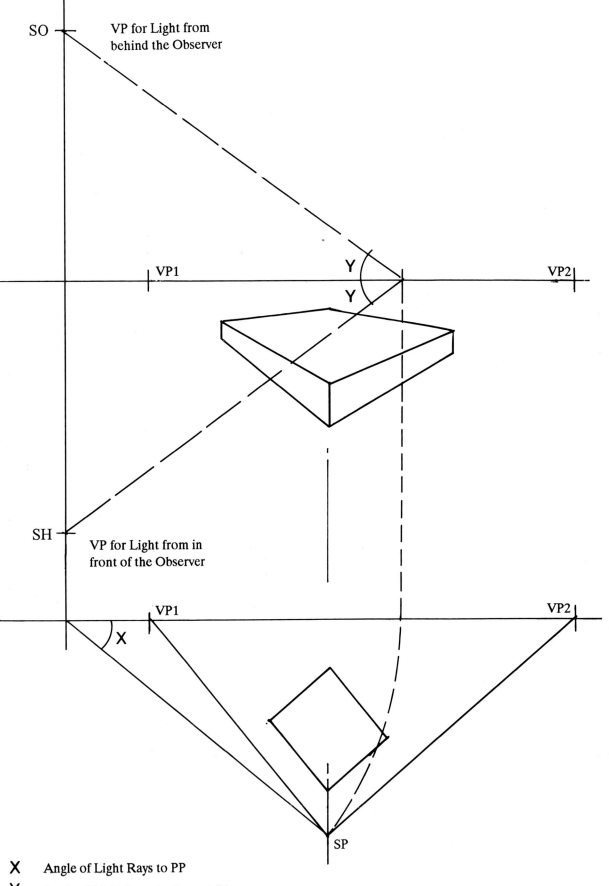

SO — VP for Light from behind the Observer

VP1 ◦ Y ◦ VP2

Y

SH — VP for Light from in front of the Observer

VP1 X VP2

SP

X   Angle of Light Rays to PP

Y   Angle of Light Rays to Ground Plane

Fig. 1.75 *Layout for the perspective construction of shadows*

56

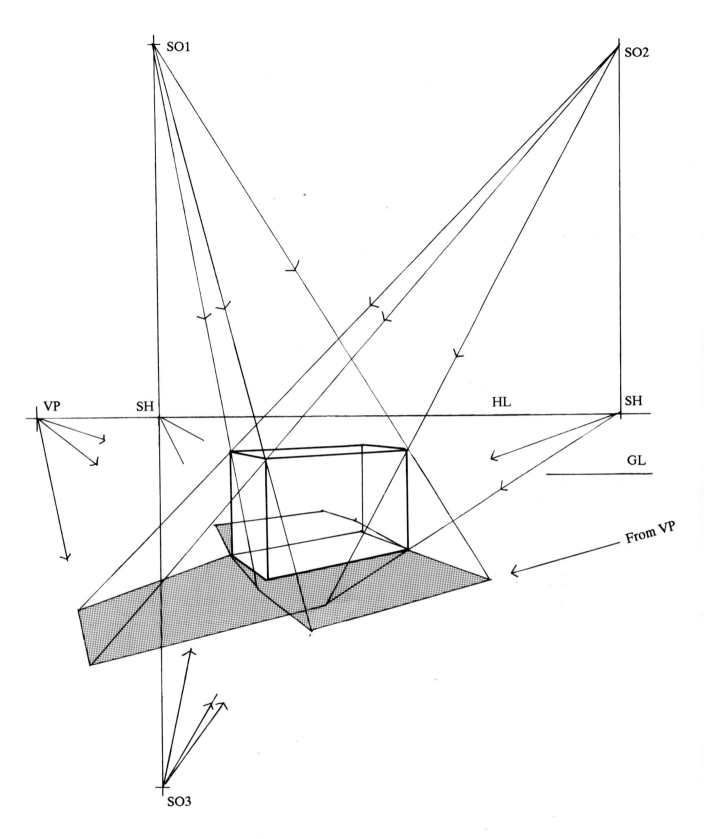

Fig. 1.76 *Sunlight parallels. Vanishing point of plane for shade lies on horizon line.*

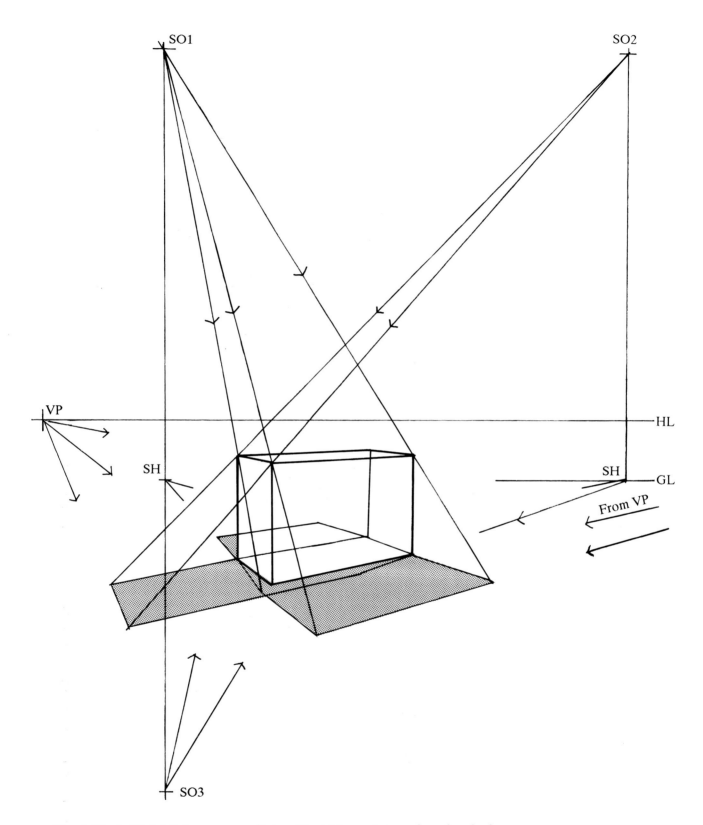

Fig. 1.77 *Artificial light source radiates. Vanishing point on plane for shade lies on ground plane*

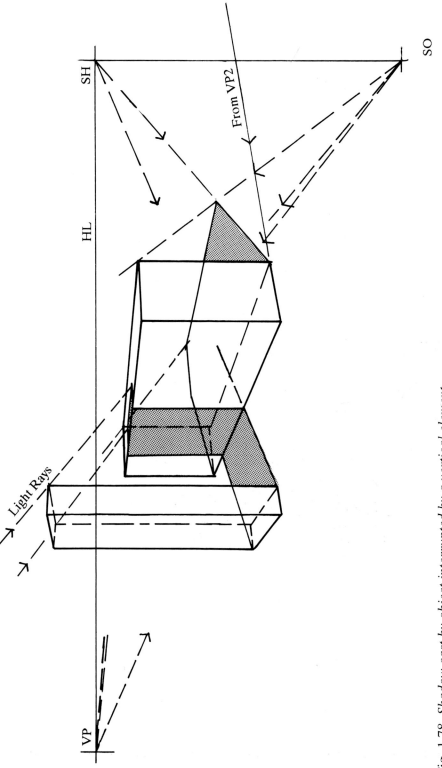

Fig. 1.78 *Shadow cast by object interrupted by a vertical element*

59

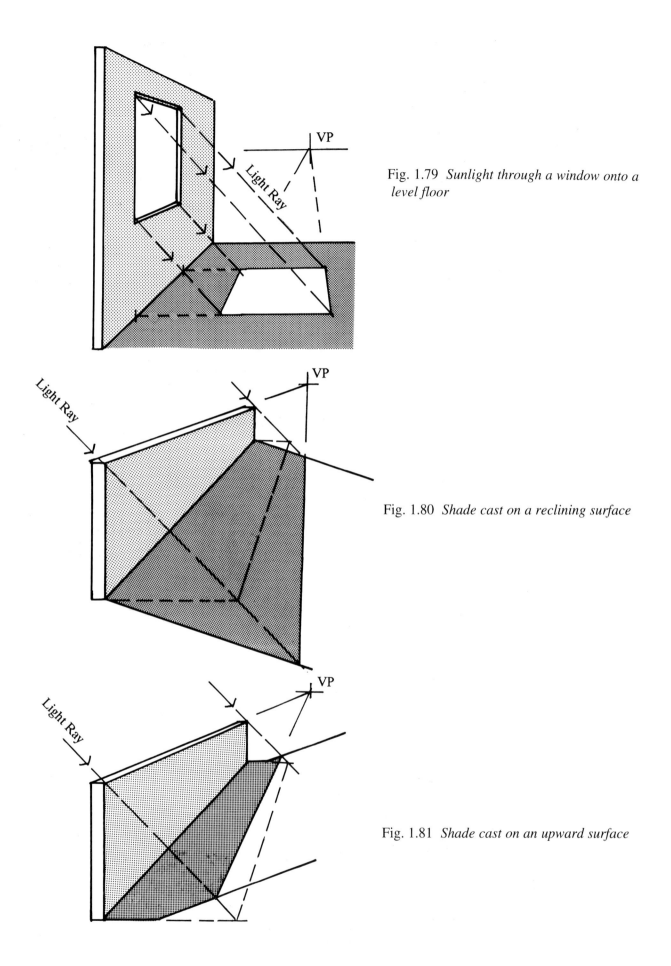

Fig. 1.79 *Sunlight through a window onto a level floor*

Fig. 1.80 *Shade cast on a reclining surface*

Fig. 1.81 *Shade cast on an upward surface*

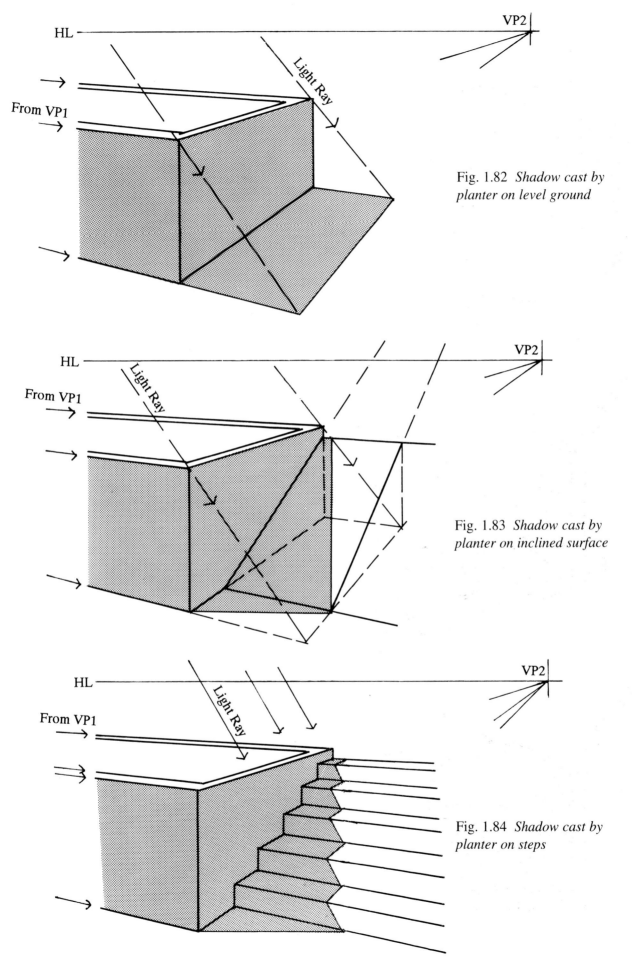

HL

VP2

From VP1

Light Ray

Fig. 1.82 *Shadow cast by planter on level ground*

HL

VP2

From VP1

Light Ray

Fig. 1.83 *Shadow cast by planter on inclined surface*

HL

VP2

From VP1

Light Ray

Fig. 1.84 *Shadow cast by planter on steps*

61

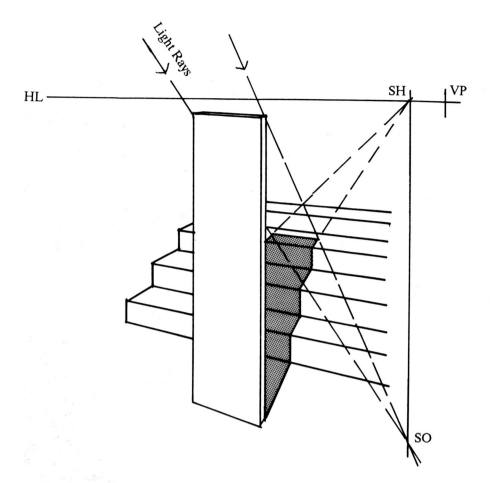

Fig. 1.85 *Light source from front of the object casts a shadow on the steps*

Fig. 1.86 *Shadow of a handrail parallel to the slope of the steps*

Fig. 1.87 *Shadow of an adjacent rising wall on steps*

Fig. 1.88 *Shadow of a vertical element adjacent to a set of steps (See Fig. 1.89)*

Fig. 1.90 *Shadow of a level planter on a set of steps. Try drawing this photo like Fig. 1.89*

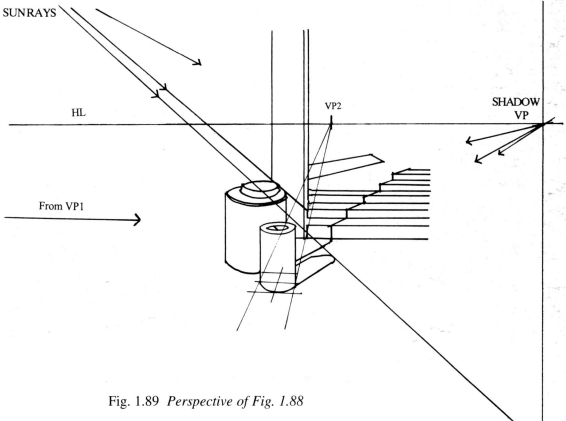

SUNRAYS

HL

From VP1

VP2

SHADOW VP

Fig. 1.89 *Perspective of Fig. 1.88*

Fig. 1.91 *Shadow of a circular brick planter on brick paving*

Fig. 1.92 *Circular shadows from lighting elements on a pedestrian ramp*

Fig. 1.93 *Shadow of a horizontal element*

Fig. 1.94 *Shadow of a vertical site element*

Fig. 1.95 *Shadows of a wheelchair ramp railing*

Fig. 1.96 *Shadows created by arched openings along a curved wall, see Fig. 1.97*

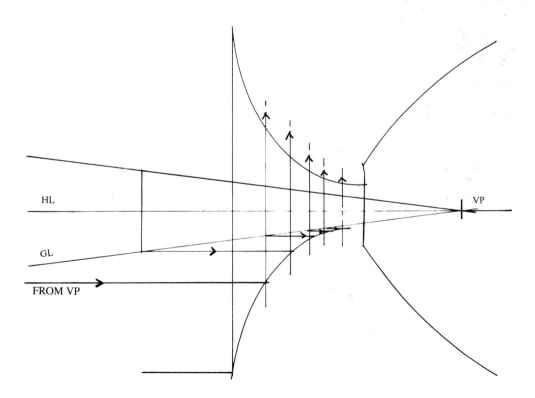

Fig. 1.97 *Perspective for Fig. 1.96*

Fig. 1.98 *Shadows from a tree on an inclined surface*

Fig. 1.99 *Shadows of trees on paving, see Fig. 1.100*

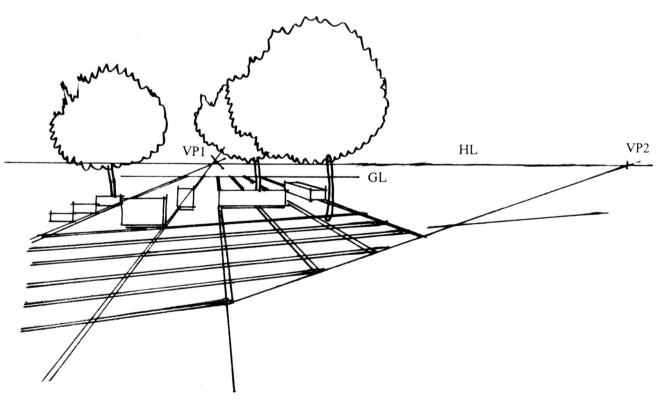

Fig. 1.100 *Perspective of Fig. 1.99*

Perspectives of Reflections

The reflection of an object will appear exactly the same as the image of the object, but opposite on the other side of the reflecting surface. Its vanishing point is the same as the object it reflects. In the case of reflection in water, the reflecting images are duplicated vertically. The reflection in the mirrored glass walls of buildings is constructed from same vanishing points. See Figures 1.102 to 1.109.

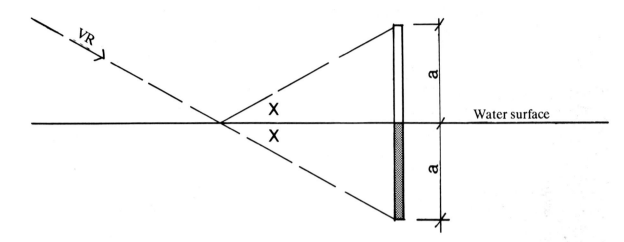

Fig. 1.101 *This diagram shows reflection angle and image from visual point*

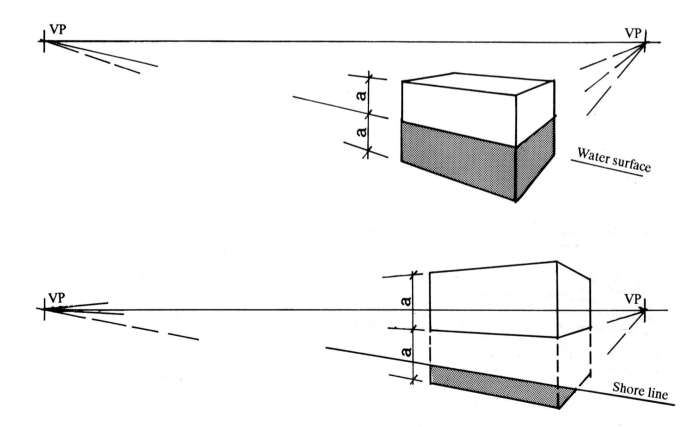

Fig. 1.102 *The reflection of an object appears in duplicate (though in reverse) on the other side of the reflecting surface*

67

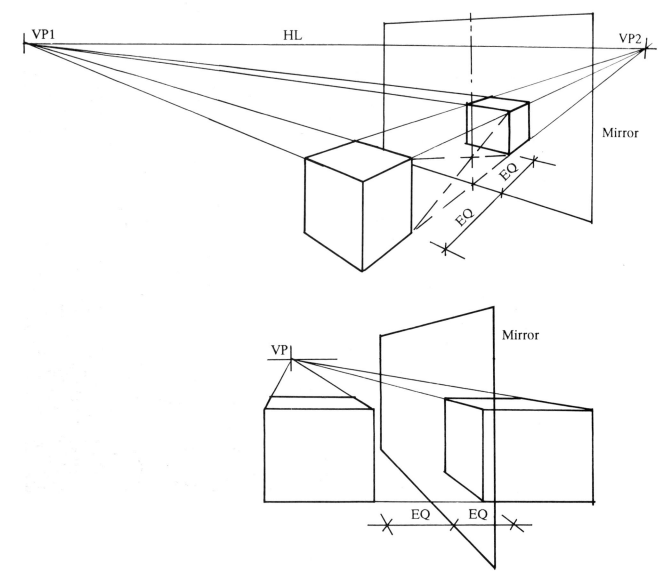

VP1   HL   VP2

Mirror

EQ   EQ

VP

Mirror

EQ   EQ

Fig. 1.103 *Mirror images are constructed by the same vanishing points as used for the object*

Fig. 1.104 *The sculpture and paving on the left are mirrored in the windows on the right*

68

Fig. 1.105 *A solid glass wall mirrors the adjacent building and trees*

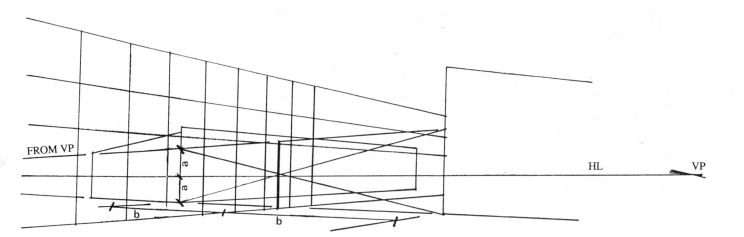

Fig. 1.106 *Perspective for Fig. 1.105*

Fig. 1.107 *Reflections of an office building in a pond*

Fig. 1.108 *Reflections of a college campus in a pond*

Fig. 1.109 *Reflections of apartment buildings and a deck (right)*

70

2

COMPOSITION

The foundation of pictorial art composition is a very complex subject. Since it is thoroughly covered in other texts, we will not discuss the subject in depth in this book, but only touch the basics. It will be helpful for you to understand the principle of linear frame work of a picture's surface, the use of color rhythms, tension and movement of lines, forms, tones and color in the process of composing an illustration for a design presentation.

There are some general rules that apply to composing an architectural illustration.

1. Placing the horizon line. The horizon line is a dominating feature as it tends to subdivide the drawing surface. Because of this, its location needs to be carefully planned. It should either be higher or lower than the center of the drawing. (See Figure 2.1)

2. Placing the object or subject. This is the second action in forming a pictorial surface. Figure 2.2 illustrates the use of a horizontal and vertical frame for the same subject. Notice how the change of frame affects the overall expression of the composition. In the vertical frame, the vertical height of the building is more intensely expressed. Conversely, the horizontal frame deemphasizes the height of the building. (See Figures 2.3)

3. Focal point. Just as a painting needs a point of emphasis, so does an architectural illustration. This is done to call attention to and demonstrate the design idea. Placing the object or subject near a central location in the composition will help attract the viewer's eye and thus becomes the focal point, or point of emphasis. (See Figures 2.4 to 2.8)

4. Planned movement. A viewer's eye tends to follow repetitive shapes or elements. By incorporating this characteristic into a composition you can provide additional reinforcement to the point of interest. Just as one strong color can call attention to the point of interest, repeating color forms along the view path can direct the viewer

to the focal point. (See Figures 2.9 to 2.14)

5. Enrichment. You can give the object or subject more emphasis by adding texture and line detail. This also creates a difference between the point of emphasis and its background thus automatically strengthening the focal point. (See Figure 2.15)

Figures 2.16 to 2.20 are some additional points to consider when composing a picture.

Fig. 2.1 *Three examples of placing the horizon line above or below the center of the drawing.*

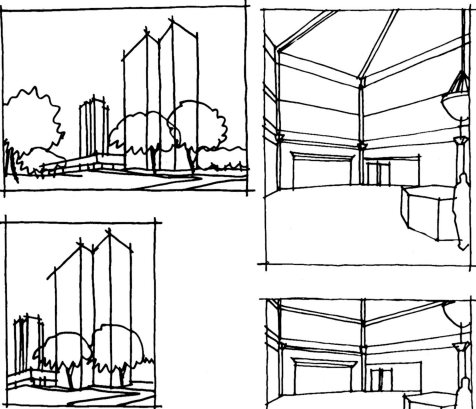

Fig. 2.2 *The difference between a horizontal and vertical frame when placing the object*

Fig. 2.3 *In interior sketching there is a difference because of the ceiling. The mood of the space changes when more of the ceiling is exposed.*

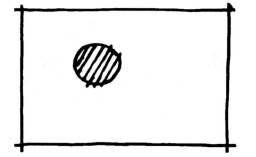

Fig. 2.4 *A single focal point can be off and near the center*

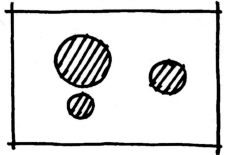

Fig. 2.5 *Place the major emphasis in a multi-focal point to the near center location*

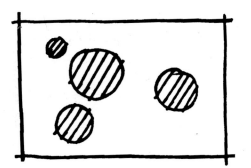

Fig. 2.6 *Maximize overall frame coverage*

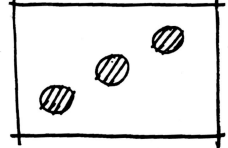

Fig. 2.7 *Repeat elements and color*

73

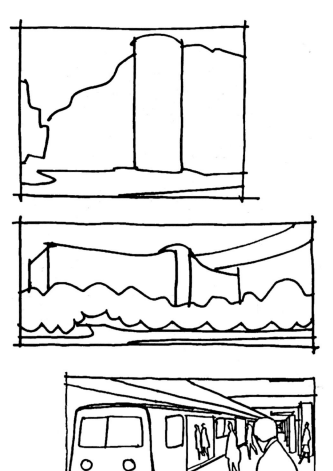

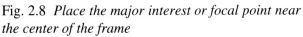

Fig. 2.10 *Overlapping suggests depth (see dashed areas)*

Main
interest
point

Close
foreground
element

Fig. 2.8 *Place the major interest or focal point near the center of the frame*

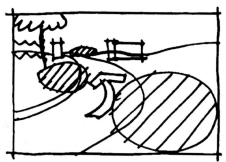

Fig. 2.9 *Grouping suggests depth (see dashed areas)*

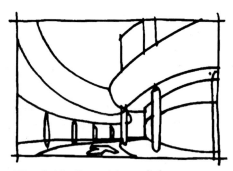

Fig. 2.11 *Repetition of shape can be used to create visual movement*

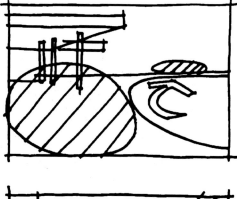

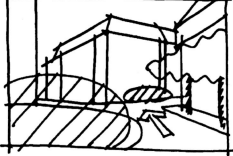

Fig. 2.13 *This sketch shows space beyond the foreground to add interest and suggests movement*

Fig. 2.12 *Create foreground and background activities for planned eye movement*

Fig. 2.14 *An example of composition. A foreground space has been formed by the three trees on the right and movement has been suggested by the curvilinear lines. A car has been added to provide scale.*

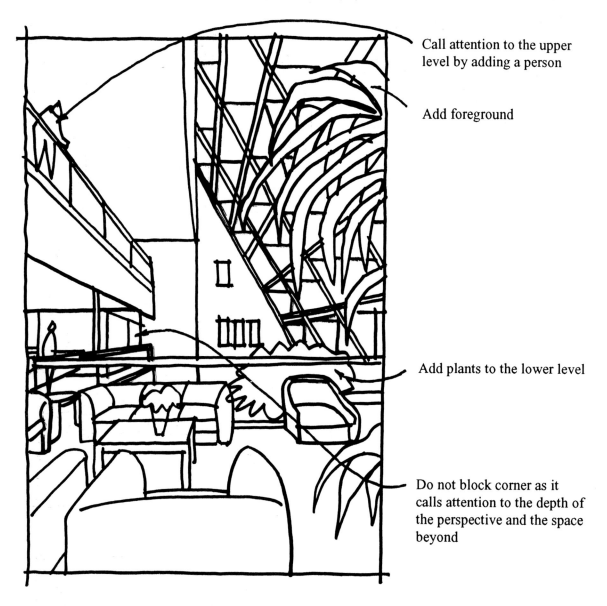

Call attention to the upper level by adding a person

Add foreground

Add plants to the lower level

Do not block corner as it calls attention to the depth of the perspective and the space beyond

Fig. 2.15 *Add elements to express level change and enrich the overall picture*

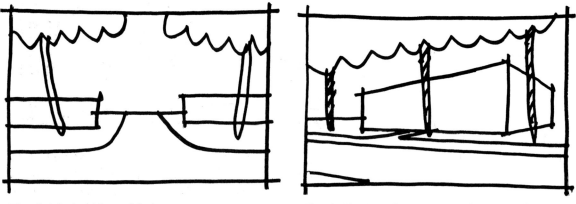

Fig. 2.16 *Avoid total balance*

Fig. 2.17 *Avoid repetition of a major line*

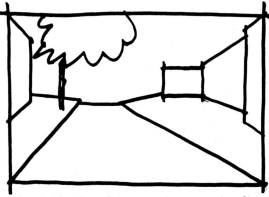

Fig. 2.18 *Avoid intersecting a major line with format corner*

Fig. 2.19 *Avoid covering a line which shows a change of direction*

Fig. 2.20 *The lines or points of space defining (the intersection) should not be all covered up (see circled areas in upper sketch). In the lower sketch most of these points have been covered up, which is to be avoided.*

3

DRAWING TECHNIQUES

LINE DRAWING

Basically a line drawing serves as a base to which either color or black and white shading or rendering is added to create a final illustration. It is also used in isometric or axonometric drawing. The uniform line weight of a line drawing tends to make it appear flat or uninteresting. The drawing can be improved by a variation in the line weight such as outlining an object, at a change of plane or using thinner lines as the distance into the perspective increases. Figure 3.1 is an example of a freehand drawing while Figure 3.2 is a hardline drawing.

TONE DRAWING

Tone is the shading of black to white much like the dark to light gray tones you see in a black and white photograph. Using dots, lines or washes can add tone to a drawing. Dots or lines can be applied either randomly in a freehand style or uniformly in hardline. Value can be accomplished by overlapping lines, or increasing the weight and/or density of lines, dots or pigment. Figure 3.4 illustrates the freehand use of overlapping lines, varying line spacing to create density, and graded weight of lines. It also shows line use variation, dot patterns and overlapping lines on a curved object.

Besides adding volume to a drawing, tone also suggests texture, value, finishes, and stimulates visual interest. Figure 3.3 is the application of overlapping and other styles of freehand lines and dots to a line drawing to create tone. Figure 3.5 is an example of irregular lines to produce tone. For an example of an ink wash to create tone, see Figure 3.6. "Zip-a-tone" is a commercially available product that features many different patterns of dots, lines, hatching, and so forth, on a transparent plastic sheet with an adhesive backing. It can be cut to fit any shape and is very useful for quickly illustrating tone.

COLOR DRAWING

The wide range of color media available today for use in architectural illustration is almost unlimited. Any particular medium can be used alone or in combination with some other medium. The possible combinations are numerous. The only limitations will be the artist's preference and style. The most common color media are as follows:

Color Pencil

Color pencil is basically transparent. It can be used over a line drawing or by itself. It gives a soft appearance and can be used on almost any paper with medium texture. The color can be built up by layers in any number of combinations to achieve the desire shade. (See Figure 3.11a and 3.11b) It is a flexible medium that is easy to control with relatively little experience. In comparison to the other media however, color pencil will not reproduce an image that is as clear and sharp when used for architectural illustrations. A layer of spray fix will increase the color intensity. Figure 3.7 is an example of a drawing with color pencil on the back of vellum while 3.9 is a wash over a black line base.

Watercolor

It is a transparent wash that can be used over a line drawing base, or it can be applied directly using the typical watercolor painting method. In either case, the application has to be on watercolor paper or board. Using a watercolor wash over a line drawn base can be simple and direct, but some practice will be required to master the use of the medium. Although the principles are the same, there is a difference between ordinary watercolor painting and architectural illustration. The wet and wet-on-wet technique common to watercolor painting is rarely used for architectural illustration that requires a precise interpretation of the object. The wet techniques produce unpredictable results. Applying watercolor with a nearly dry technique is more successful; color is built-up to achieve the desired shade.

Transferring the line drawn base to watercolor paper can be tedious work and time consuming. So, a preplanned color scheme will be helpful to avoid a lot of redoing. Since color correction would be difficult without color build-up, the end result could appear muddy and unappealing. Transferring the base can be done in a specialized printing shop and is called blueline board, which is quite expensive. Other transfer methods involve using a light table or a graphite sheet. Watercolor paper of any brand should be 140lb or heavier, prestretched, cold or hot pressed, and medium texture. See Figure 3.8 for an example of a watercolor illustration.

Glazing. A thin transparent wash applied over dried washes enriches the color. The transparent coating gives an added depth to the original color underneath. Generally, three applications of glaze are the limit. With more than three layers, the glaze loses its transparency and the color begins to look muddy.

Masking. There may be a need at time to produce a crisp, hard edge. This can be done by using masking tape, commercial graphics designer tape, or liquid frisket.

Tapes come in different widths, but masking tape does not give complete satisfaction. Frisket works better and is a commercially available material of paper or plastic with adhesive backing that is available in sheets of rolls or liquid masking. Place a frisket sheet or liquid over the area to be masked and cut precisely to fit. Practice using masking materials before launching into a final project.

Irregular edge. The edges of plants or cloud patterns are irregular and soft. This effect can be achieved by using a wash or airbrush over a piece of torn tissue paper or cotton.

Splatters. Soak an old toothbrush with color and rub it across a piece of screen or run your finger across the bristles directing the splatters onto the paper. This creates an irregular series of spots or dots that can be quite effective to represent textures and finishes. Mask areas with torn or cut paper to control the shapes you desire.

Washes. An even or graded wash is a technique quite often used to create a sky. The area to be washed should be masked as described above, and pre-wetted. For a graded wash, begin where the color should be the darkest. Using color, carefully brush downward away from the darkest area to create a uniform grade from dark to light.

Corrections. Excess color and water may be lifted by using dry tissue paper or a brush while the surface is still wet.

Markers

Markers have improved considerably over the past decade and are now available in over 150 colors with varying tip width. They have been widely used by design professionals, are easy to use and require no mixing or cleanup. They produce intense color and the colors can be overlapped. Because they dry fast they are time saving as overlay color can be applied immediately. Most papers can be used except those that are very smooth.

Some practice in the use of markers is advisable because mistakes are difficult to cover or change. The width of the tip creates a stroke mark. The amount of the mark will vary by paper type. It will be necessary to test the papers you want to use before proceeding, especially if you want to express a curved volume where stroke marks will interfere with the effect you want to create. See Figures 3.12 and 3.13 for marker examples.

Felt-tip Pens

Similar to markers, felt-tip pens have a thin tip in comparison to the large felt-tips of markers. There are many brand names and colors available. These pens are best used for adding details and lines where needed in a drawing. (See Figure 3.10)

Acrylic, Casein or Tempera

Acrylics are compatible with a wide variety of surfaces and are simple to use. The application techniques are similar to watercolor as already described above. They also can be used as an opaque medium.

Air Brush

Air brushing is a technique of applying color with a pressurized spray, creating either a transparent or opaque layer depending upon the media being used. The medium can be ink, watercolor, gouache or acrylics and etc. Generally, watercolor paper or illustration board is suitable. The use of an air brush is complicated and requires considerable patience, practice and planning. There are marker type sprays available in a compressed air can that are convenient and can be used where a coarser result is desired. (See Figure 3.15)

Pastel

Pastels are made of compressing chalk and pigment. There are hard and soft pastel sticks available. The hardness is dependent upon the percentage of binding material each contains. *Ingres* paper is most commonly used for pastels, but any other paper with texture can be used. Mistakes can be easily lifted with a kneaded eraser and then corrected. A thin layer of fixative spray will help keep the pastel in place and preserve it. Pastel drawing tends to be coarse and difficult to use in a detail drawing. Color pencils can be used for some of the detail work. Other combinations can be explored, and you may want to experiment. (See Figure 3.14)

COMBINATIONS

A combination of the media previously described is often used to achieve the best result. Each medium has its advantages and disadvantages. Used together they can complement each other. For instance, color pencil can be used with a marker to express the softness the marker cannot achieve by itself. Creating tone by using a wash over an inkline drawing will add richness to an illustration. The combinations are endless. Explore the possibilities by experimentation and practice, and select the technique and medium combinations that work best for you. (See Figure 5.38 on page 186)

DETAIL ELEMENTS

SKY

A large portion of most illustrations will be occupied by the sky, especially if the illustration features a single object such as a building or a park. It is therefore desirable to plan carefully the sky's color, form and technique before beginning.

Since a sky serves as a background in an architectural illustration, it is different from a painting where the artist tries to capture the existing image. The sky is part of the total composition and should be complementary rather than competing with the other parts such as a building or space. The color or form of the sky should not dominate.

Painting the sky is usually the first step as it establishes the basic value for the rest of the composition. This does not always have to be the case however, and the sky can be completed at any time while doing the illustration. It all depends upon the efficient use of your time and what works best for you under the circumstances.

The principle of perspective applies to the composition of the sky. Clouds become smaller in the distance and the color of the sky fades away toward the distant horizon.

A well balanced sky composition can enhance an illustration and create a mood. A blue sky presents a pleasant atmosphere. It can become more dramatic with the addition of clouds. You can draw attention to a peak of or define a building, and express height as well as distance.

The colors you select for painting a sky should be compatible and harmonize with the overall color scheme. It should not in any way overpower the subject of the composition. When working with watercolor consider using cerulean blue, or warm gray. If a warm color is needed you might try using windsor yellow or alizarin crimson. A graded wash or flat wash are the techniques most commonly used for both watercolor and airbrush illustration of the sky. Sponge wet the entire surface to be painted, apply blue, and tilt the paper or board until you have a perfect graded wash. Frisk can be used to mask the area of the object. Lightly sketch the clouds, paint the blue portion of the sky and wait for it to dry. Then, add shade to the clouds to express the three dimension, and soften the edges by using a damp brush. Another technique is to paint the entire sky and before it is dry use a sponge or tissue paper to lift the blue from the areas where you want to show clouds.

When using an airbrush, the surface area does not need to be wet. A softened and irregular edge can be achieved by holding some torn tissue paper or cotton in the left hand and move it along while spraying with the right hand.

Color pencils can be used for painting a sky. There are several shades of blue, warm gray, yellow, orange, sand, light flesh, and others that can be utilized. Pencils have increased in popularity since they facilitate a soft touch, and a low key appearance. The color can be built-up by layering, and it is erasable to a certain extent, depending upon the type of paper you selected. It is possible to use a combination of media for painting a sky including watercolor/color pencil or inkline/color pencil.

Markers can be a time saving choice, but the color tends to be intense. As previously recommended, test and practice with the medium before using it. The strokes from the marker tip will remain so it will require some effort to master the technique to minimize the problem. Markers do not allow the range of color choices available for pencils or watercolor. It is easy to create a muddy appearance by overlayering.

For black and white illustration of sky, the use of lines and stipples is effective. Plan ahead for the composition of the sky in relationship to the overall drawing, including the placement of clouds and the use of tone. Remember to keep it simple so as not to overpower the subject. (See Figures 3.15 to 3.20)

HUMAN FIGURES, VEHICLES, FURNITURE, WATER

Serving a support function in an illustration are human figures, furniture, automobiles, planters, etc. These items help to visualize the space or environment and humanize the picture being created. They help to demonstrate the use of space and indicate the scale of the project, the ground form, levels and so forth.

The following is a list of guidelines for adding these elements in an illustration:

* Act as a "balance force" to the overall composition.

* Grouping or overlapping suggest depth in the space.

* Detail should be kept to a minimum so as not to overpower the subject.

* Where there is a continuation of spaces, the line of space defining the intersection should not be covered.

* Color should harmonize with the overall color scheme. Use of minimum of accent to call the attention of the viewer.

* Close-up foreground elements are often used in architectural illustration to bring the viewer into the picture, such as a human figure in the foreground. Another is the placement of a canopy of a tree under which the viewer sees the space beyond.

* Support elements must create a setting, as a force toward the center of interest, such as adding human figures going into and coming out of the entrance will draw attention to that space.

Interior illustration is more difficult to plan and time consuming because it involves more details. Some of these, such as overlapping elements, textures, finishes, and lighting effects are different from exterior illustration. Artificial light sources are usually multiple so that the edge of shading is soft. Some pre-planning is required in order to select the best view point, angle and interest position.

Because adding human figures, automobiles, furniture, plants and other details to the base illustration is very time consuming, it is very helpful to develop a resource file. There are many illustration resource books available in bookstores. In addition you will find it useful to collect pictures from newspapers, and magazines. A camera is a valuable collecting tool. Taking slides of various details and elements makes it easy to project those images at just the right size onto your project for tracing.

Drawing human figures, furniture, and so forth, in an illustration requires that you follow the same perspective base by constructing boxes, see Figures 3.21 to 3.41.

Plants

Plants are important elements in both interior and exterior illustrations. Plant materials include trees, shrubs, groundcovers, and flowers. They can be used in a sketch to:

* frame the picture (See Figure 3.42)

* use as balancing in the composition (See Figure 3.43)

* emphasize a focal point (See Figure 3.44)

* cover an unwanted detail such as an undesirable corner (See Figure 3.45)

* add texture to the illustration (See Figure 3.46)

* create a pleasant atmosphere (See Figure 3.47)

To develop your drawing techniques, start by observing plants in your everyday surroundings. Look at their growth habits, branching structure, and texture. Collecting photographs or pictures will allow you to bring what you see back into the studio for additional study and sketching. In the beginning practice by tracing pictures of single plants and then groups. (See Figures 3.48, 3.53, 3.55 - 3.58)

The scale of a plant is important. The size is determined by both its natural growth habit and its relationship to the overall composition. A plant that is drawn too large or too small damages the composition. (See Figure 3.50) Plants used in interior illustrations are typically drawn with considerable detail as very specific types are used in the composition. They are viewed very close in comparison to exterior illustrations. (See Figures 3.51 and 3.52)

When drawing plants, the continuation of the branching structure as well as the leaf mass is essential to express fully the three dimensions of the tree. Shading with the leaf mass adds to the three dimensional feeling. The most difficult part is to draw the branches that extend toward you, but it is very important because these give the composition a three dimensional effect. In many cases they become the foreground of your sketch. (See Figure 3.49)

It is important to change the shape, height and distance of trees on groupings in order to reflect correctly the principles of perspective. (See Figure 3.54) Not all trees grow straight out of the ground. As you draw them, keep this in mind and allow some to be at an angle just like they are in nature. (See Figures 3.56 to 3.58)

Figures 3.59 to 3.61 are some examples of how to improve perspectives by adding plants and some poorly composed perspectives in relationship to tree placement.

For shading you can use the same method by tracing photographs and study the shade of leaf mass before rendering. (See Figures 3.62 to 3.65). Shadows of plants that are cast upon the ground, water or snow, or against such vertical elements as walls, or furniture, all add to the dimension and interest of the perspective. (See Figures 3.66 to 3.68 for photos of trees that cast interesting shadows.)

Size and texture of plants diminishes from the foreground to the background in the same relationship to the vanishing points as the rest of the objects in the sketch. (See Figure 3.70) The amount of texture you draw is dependent upon the viewing distance. For sketches where you are close to more detail, texture will be drawn. (See Figure 3.69) In compositions with greater distance, less texture will appear and plant shapes or forms and groupings will become more important. (See Figures 3.71 to 3.72)

Texture can be observed in a plant in several ways. During the winter when the foliage is off, the texture might be expressed by the branching pattern. Heavy thick branches might be classified as a coarse texture whereas a plant with many small branches close together could be referred to as having a fine texture. During the summer when the leaves are in place, texture might be expressed by the size and spacing of the leaves. Large leaves and loose branches would define a coarse texture. Small leaves and closely spaced branches represent a fine texture. (See Figures 3.73 to 3.79)

After preparing the basic perspective, the rendering of plants helps to make the drawing complete and more interesting. For photographs and examples of rendering techniques of tree branches and trunks, see Figures 3.80 to 3.85.

Color can be added to the plants in a perspective to complement and harmonize with the rest of the drawing. This means that the color does not necessarily have to be green. The color added does need to be compatible. The paper that is used and the medium selected will help dictate your rendering technique and vice versa. Some pre-planning will be required as discussed in Section 3. (See Figures 3.86 to 3.87)

Fig. 3.1 *Example of freehand line*

Fig. 3.2 *Example of a hard line drawing*

Fig. 3.3 *Tone drawing using lines and dots*

Tone value can be accomplished by

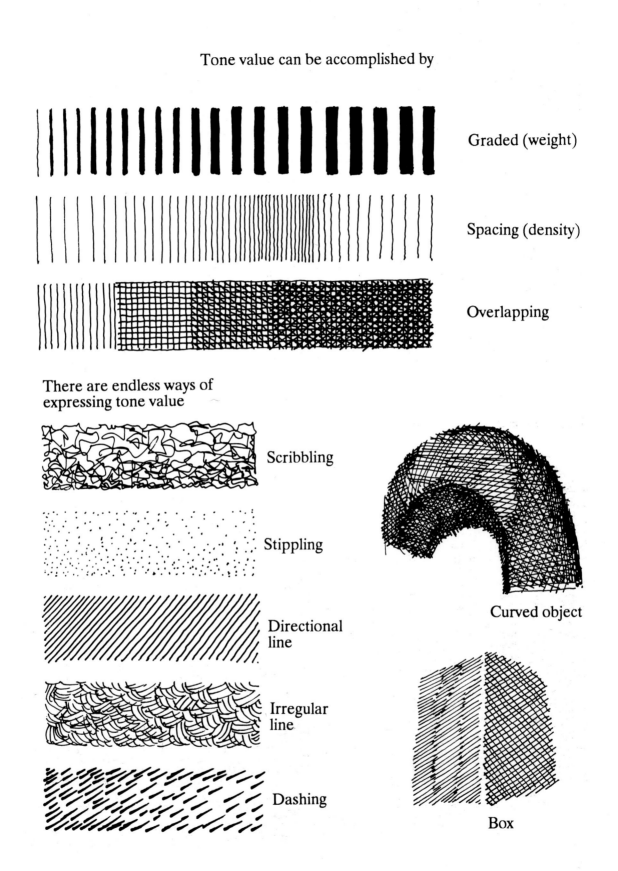

Graded (weight)

Spacing (density)

Overlapping

There are endless ways of
expressing tone value

Scribbling

Stippling

Directional
line

Irregular
line

Dashing

Curved object

Box

Fig. 3.4 *Example of a tone drawing. Freehand shading creates different effects
than hard line*

Fig. 3.5 *Tone drawing with freehand irregular lines*

Fig. 3.6 *Tone drawing with an ink wash*

88

Fig. 3.7 *Ink line on vellum with color pencil on the back*

Fig. 3.8 *Watercolor on 140lb. hot press watercolor paper. Original size: 10" x 14"*

Fig. 3.9 *Ink line base and color pencil on photographic paper. Original size: 11 1/2" x 29"*

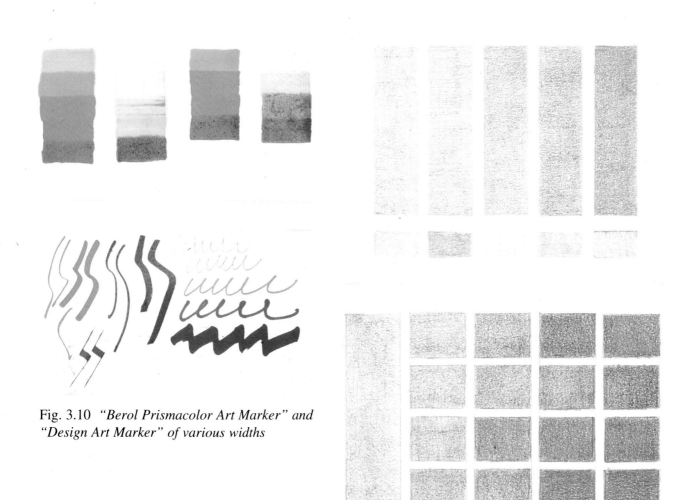

Fig. 3.10 *"Berol Prismacolor Art Marker" and "Design Art Marker" of various widths*

Fig. 3.11a *An example of color layering by "Berol Prismacolor" pencil. See Figure 3.11b for key*

Fig. 3.12 *Marker on tracing paper. Original size: 18" x 24"*

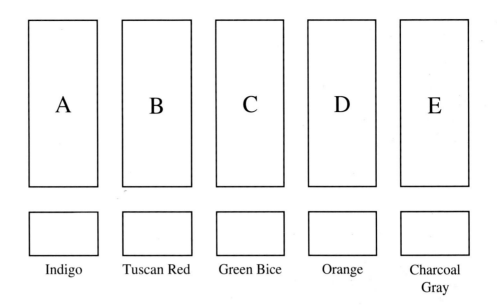

Indigo   Tuscan Red   Green Bice   Orange   Charcoal Gray

"Berol Prismacolor" Indigo Blue was applied on A to E (large top rectangles). Then areas B through E were covered with Tuscan Red. Areas C through E were covered with Green Bice, and areas D and E were covered with Orange. Finally, E was covered with Charcoal Gray. (Small rectangles indicate the five colors used.) Notice that the color variation is unlimited.

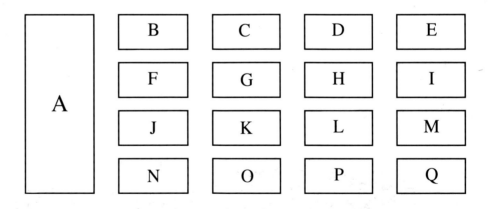

To areas A through Q, "Berol Prismacolor" Copenhagen Blue was applied. To areas B through E, White was applied; F through I, Cream was applied; J through M, Flesh was applied; and N through Q, Warm Gray was applied. To rectangles C, G, K, and O, additional Copenhagen Blue was applied, and the process repeated in the rectangles to the right. Notice the increase in color intensity. When each layer is blended and smoothed, it gives the surface a glazed effect.

Fig. 3.11b *Key to Figure 3.11a, color layering*

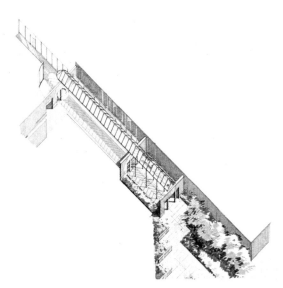

Fig. 3.13 *An example of an isometric. Marker on black line print. Original size: 24" x 24"*

Fig. 3.15 *An example of pastel drawing*

Fig. 3.14 *Air brush with ink line on vellum*

92

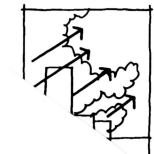
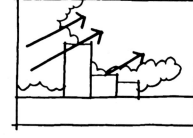
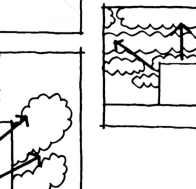

Fig. 3.16a *Examples of layouts of clouds in the sky for perspective illustrations. Follow the same principles of perspective theory*

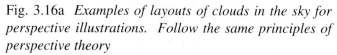

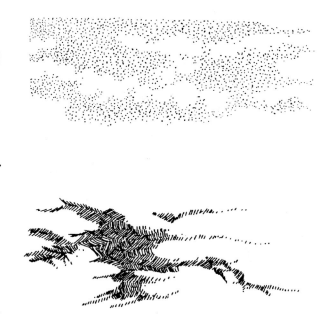

Fig. 3.16b *Try drawing this sky using one of the techniques illustrated on this page*

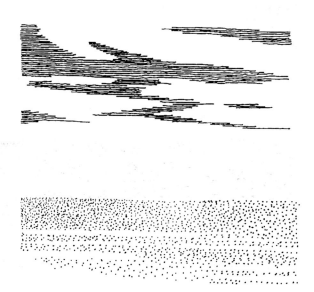

Fig. 3.17 *Examples of sky rendering with ink*

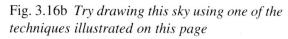

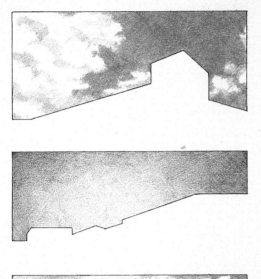

Fig. 3.19 *Graded air brush spray that can be used to render a sky*

Fig. 3.18 *Sky examples rendered with color pencil on 140lb. hot press watercolor paper*

Fig. 3.20 *Try drawing this photo and rendering the sky with one of the techniques illustrated on this page, or page 93*

Fig. 3.21 *Human figures rendered in watercolor except two (lower left) figures which are color pencil*

Typical One Head Length

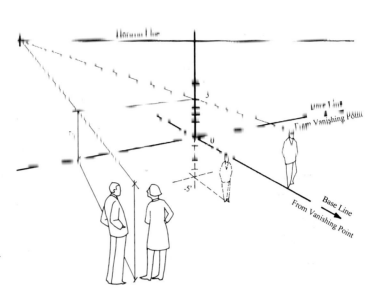

Fig. 3.22 *Proportion varies as much as people do. However, the classical method is using heads-length as the unit of measurement. In nature, the average figure height is between seven and eight heads.*

Fig. 3.23 *Aerial view of human figures in two-point perspective construction*

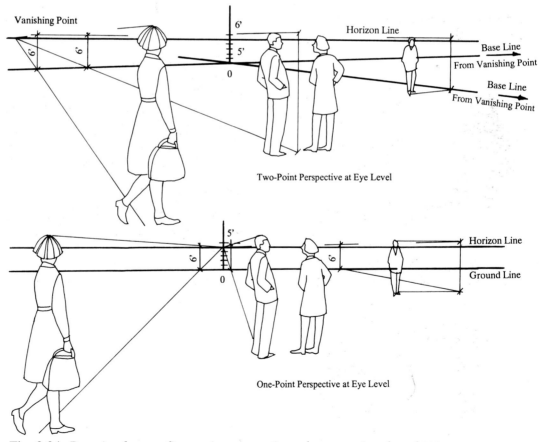

Two-Point Perspective at Eye Level

One-Point Perspective at Eye Level

Fig. 3.24 *Drawing human figures in perspective: always project from base*

95

Fig. 3.25 *Examples of human figures at eye level*

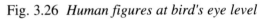

Fig. 3.26 *Human figures at bird's eye level*

Fig. 3.27a *Human figures rendered with ink line*

Fig, 3.27b *Human figures rendered with ink line*

Fig. 3.28 *Examples of water rendered with ink line*

Fig. 3.29 *Reflection in water rendered with air brush on vellum*

Fig. 3.31 *Cars rendered in watercolor (top), marker (middle), and color pencil (bottom)*

Fig. 3.30 *Watercolor with ink line on vellum*

Fig. 3.32 *Furniture rendering using color pencil (top), watercolor (middle), and marker (bottom). See page 103*

99

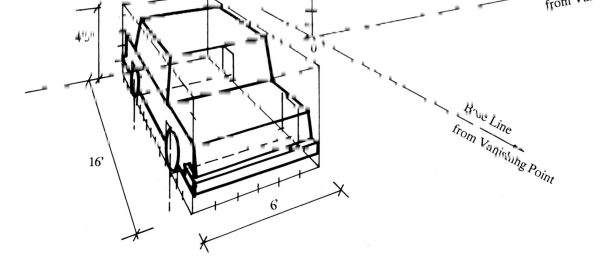

Fig. 3.33 *Aerial view of a car in two-point perspective*

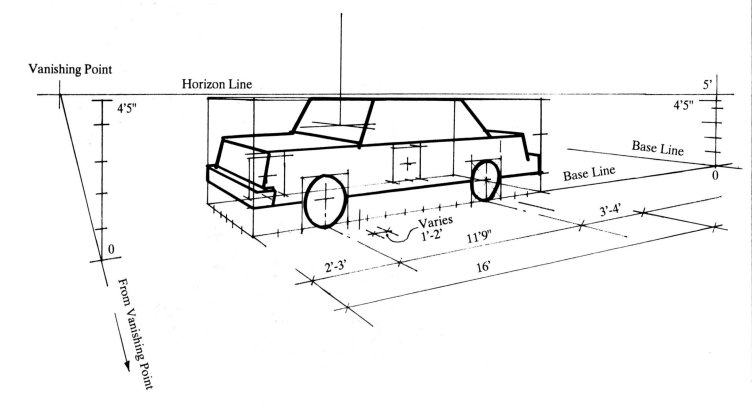

Fig. 3.34 *Eye level view of a car in two-point perspective*

Fig. 3.35 *Examples of vehicles drawn freehand and rendered with ink line*

Fig. 3.36 *Examples of vehicles from various view angles and levels*

Fig. 3.37 *Vehicles rendered with ink line*

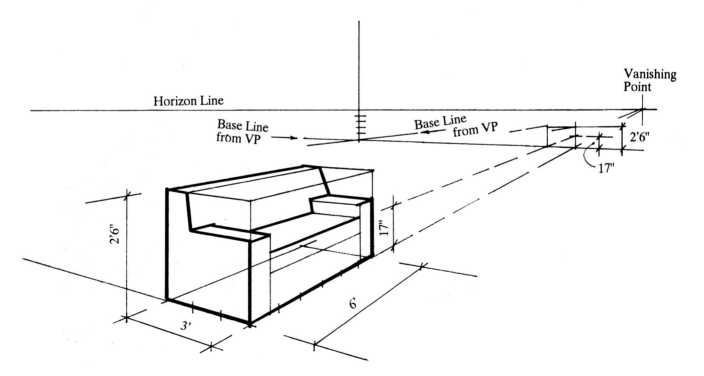

Fig. 3.38 *Eye level view of furniture in two-point perspective*

102

Fig. 3.39 *Eye level view of furniture rendered in ink line*

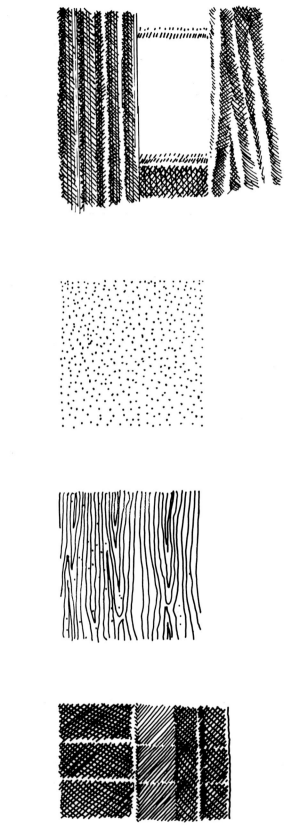

Fig. 3.40 *Examples of ink rendered finishes*

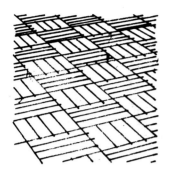
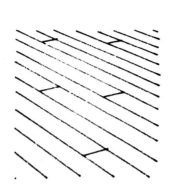

Fig. 3.42 *Trees used to frame a picture*

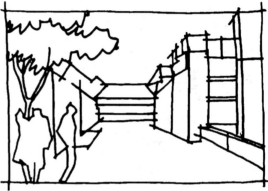

Fig. 3.43 *A tree used as a balancing element in the composition*

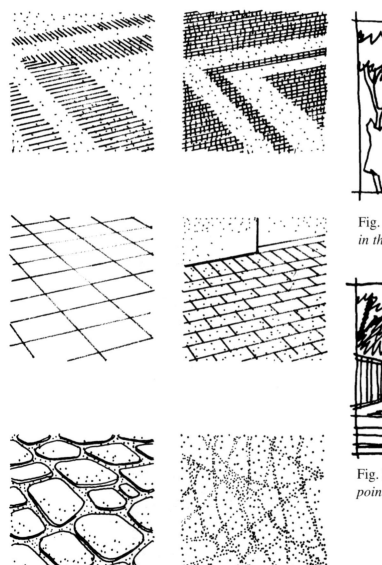

Fig. 3.44 *Trees assist in emphasizing a focal point*

Fig. 3.41 *Examples of ink rendered finishes and textures*

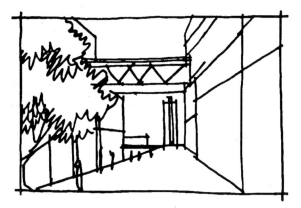

Fig. 3.45 *A tree is used to cover an unwanted detail such as the end of the bridge*

Fig. 3.46 *Plants add texture to a picture*

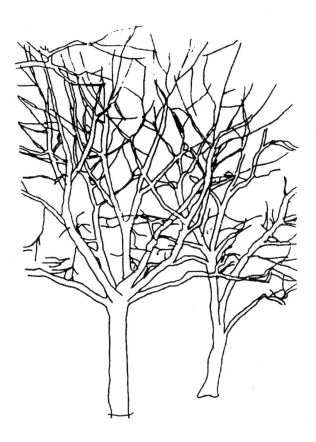

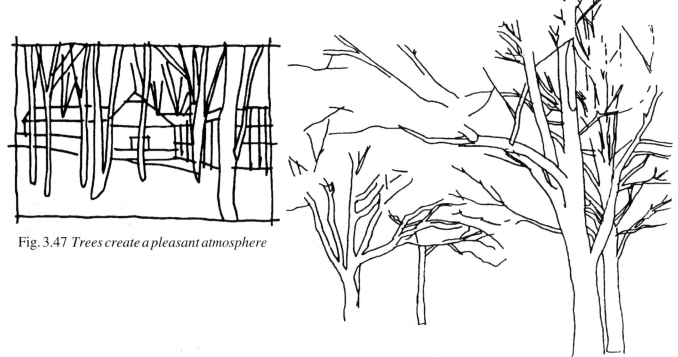

Fig. 3.47 *Trees create a pleasant atmosphere*

Fig. 3.48 *Practice tracing the trees above to get a feel of the branching habit and pattern*

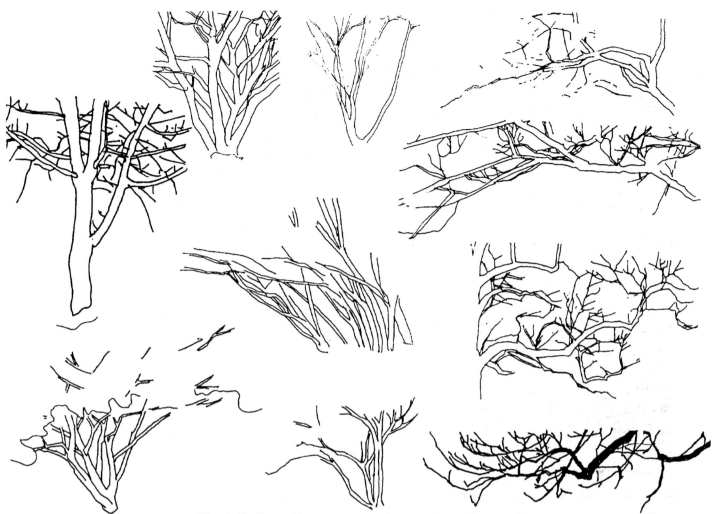

Fig. 3.49 *Branching structure of trees. Notice how each branch becomes smaller as it reaches the upper or outer end*

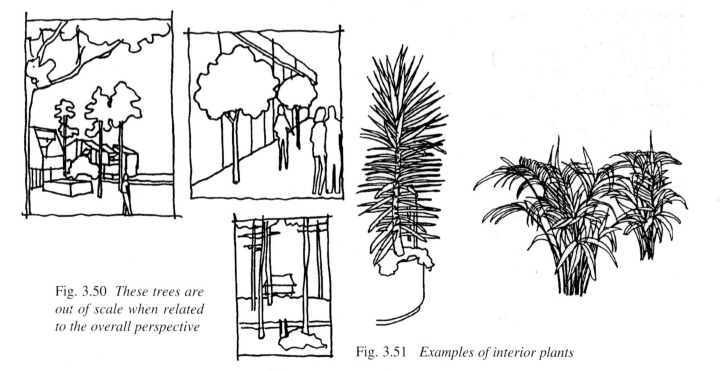

Fig. 3.50 *These trees are out of scale when related to the overall perspective*

Fig. 3.51 *Examples of interior plants*

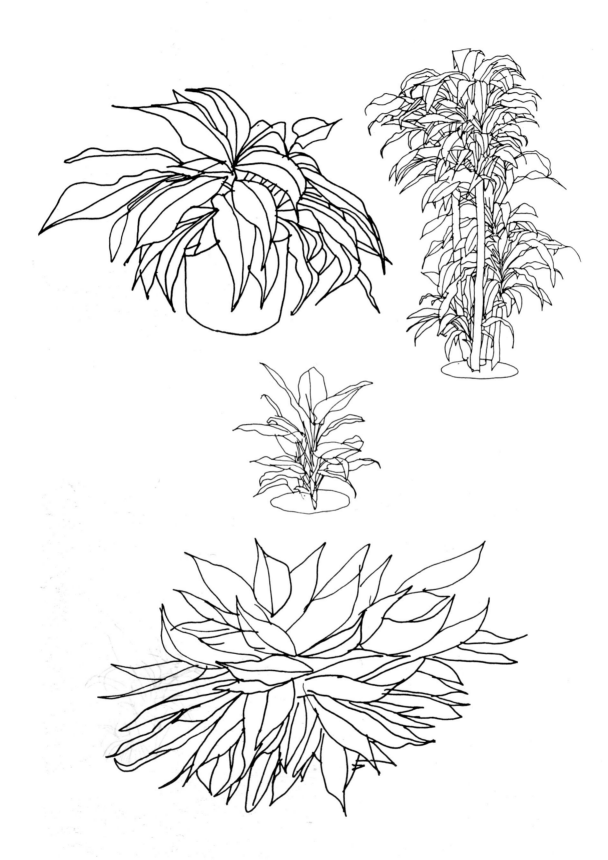

Fig. 3.52 *Examples of interior plants*

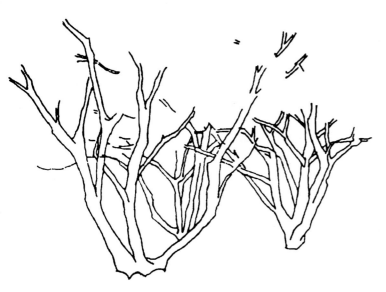

Fig. 3.53 *The multiple use of one branch structure by tracing it again and again. By reducing or reversing the image, and grouping it, you can fit it into the overall composition of the illustration.*

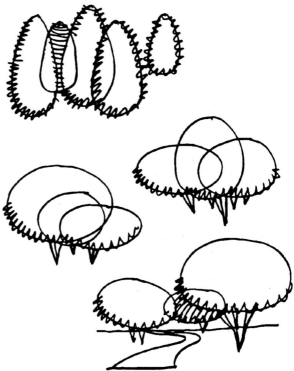

Fig. 3.54 *Vary the shape, height and placement of plants in forming a picture frame*

Fig. 3.55 *Practice by drawing or tracing the branching patterns in these photographs*

Fig. 3.56 *Multiple trunk trees*

Fig. 3.57 *Ink sketch of Fig. 3.56*

Fig. 3.58 *For practice, draw these four photographs. See Figures 3.56 and 3.57*

112

Fig. 3.59 *Improve the top sketches by adding trees, which creates depth*

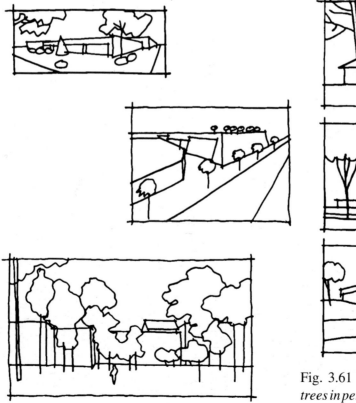

Fig. 3.60 *(top) Avoid spotty placement of plants; (middle) avoid repetition of a strong diagonal line; (bottom) groupings of plants are best*

Fig. 3.61 *Examples of poorly placed trees in perspective view. The top sketch is too symmetrical, the middle lacks interest, and the bottom is too spotty.*

Fig. 3.62 *Study the shade effects from this photo-graph and draw similar to Figure 3.63*

light   shade area

Fig. 3.63 *A technique for evaluating the light and shade areas of vegetation. Block the shade area to express depth*

Fig. 3.64 *Study the shade effects from this photograph and draw similar to Figure 3.63*

114

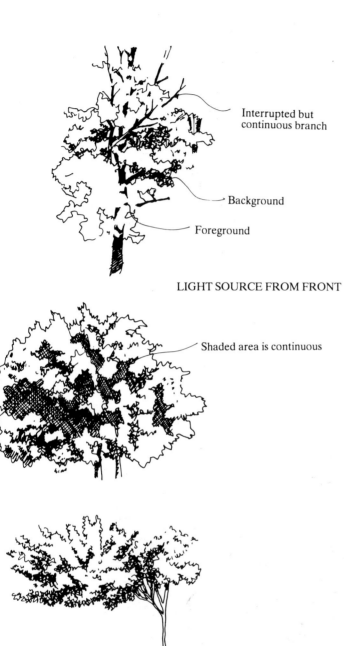

Interrupted but
continuous branch

Background

Foreground

LIGHT SOURCE FROM FRONT

Shaded area is continuous

LIGHT SOURCE FROM RIGHT

Fig. 3.65 *Technique for rendering trees and their shady areas*

Fig. 3.66 *Study the shadow patterns on the pavement beneath the trees*

Fig. 3.67 *Drawing for Figure 3.68*

Fig. 3.68 *Shadows of branches on the snow*

Fig. 3.69 *Close-up detail. Add texture and shading*

Fig. 3.70 *Detail of trees diminishes as the distance increases*

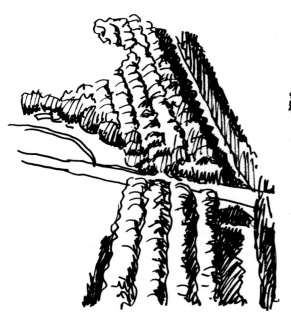

Fig. 3.71 *Large scale aerial view*

Fig. 3.74 *Aerial view of planting*

Fig. 3.72 *Light, simple textured tree in aerial view*

Fig. 3.75 *One of many techniques for drawing trees*

Fig. 3.73 *Fine textured plant*

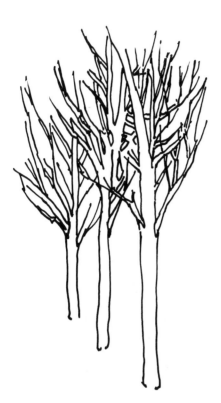

Fig. 3.76 *Coarse textured tree*

Fig. 3.77 *Fine textured tree*

Fig. 3.78 *Texture drawing for Figure 3.79*

Fig. 3.79 *Varying texture and depth as well as interest*

Freehand lines

Cross hatching

Coarse Texture

Short strokes

Fig. 3.80 *Simple and time saving techniques for drawing trees*

Fig. 3.81 *Drawing of bark texture in Figure 3.82*

Fig. 3.82 *Example of bark texture*

Fig. 3.83 *Drawing of bark texture in Figure 3.84*

Fig. 3.84 *Bark texture of a tree*

120

Fig. 3.85 *Draw the texture of these bark photos similar to Figures 3.81 and 3.83*

Fig. 3.86 *Tree branches and leaves were rendered with color pencil and ink line (top). An interior plant was rendered with marker and ink line (bottom).*

Fig. 3.87 *The top tree was rendered in watercolor on 140lb. hot press watercolor paper while the bottom tree was done in watercolor with ink line on vellum*

4

CONSTRUCTING A PERSPECTIVE

STEP BY STEP EXAMPLES

In this section five projects are presented that illustrate the step by step methods of constructing perspectives. Each project is different to give you almost the full range of possibilities. These include:

Project No. 1, a one-point perspective of a pedestrian plaza (using Lawson Perspective Chart #8),

Project No. 2, a two-point perspective of a shopping center (using Lawson Perspective Chart #6),

Project No. 3, a bird's-eye perspective for the renovation of a building complex (using Lawson Perspective Chart #1),

Project No. 4, using a slide to construct a perspective for an addition to an existing building,

Project No. 5, an example of two-point perspective (30°/60°) construction of an octagon building lobby by freehand.

PROJECT 1

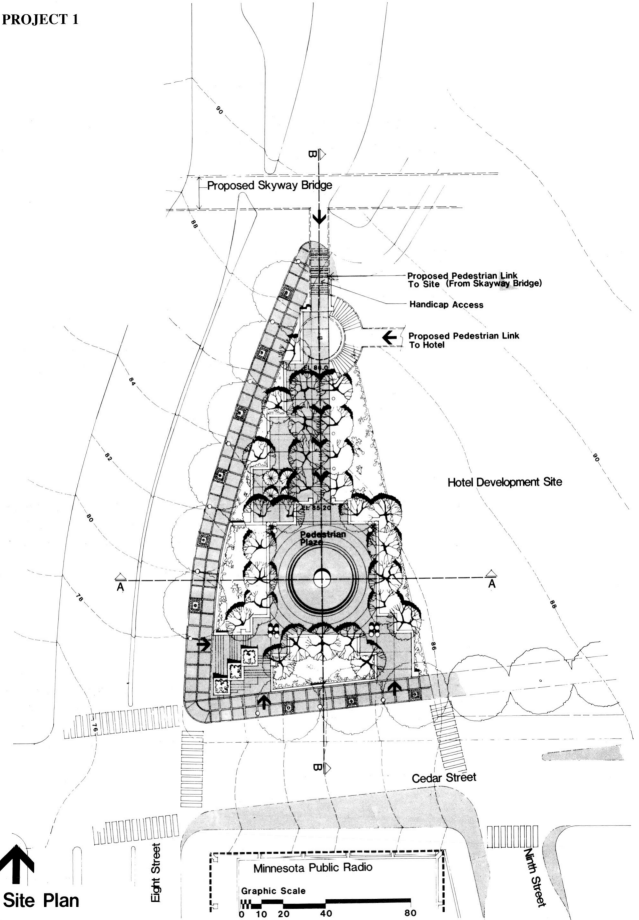

Proposed Skyway Bridge

Proposed Pedestrian Link
To Site (From Skayway Bridge)

Handicap Access

Proposed Pedestrian Link
To Hotel

Hotel Development Site

Pedestrian Plaza

A — A

B — B

Cedar Street

Eight Street

North Street

Minnesota Public Radio

Graphic Scale

0   10 20   40   80

Site Plan

Fig. 4.1 *Project No. 1, Step 1, secure a site plan to start*

124

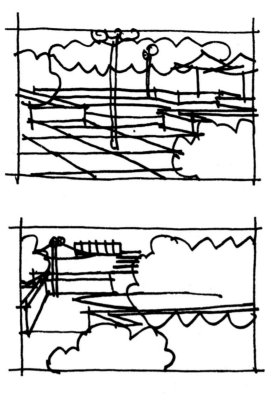

View 1

It shows only a limited area and will be good for a second support perspective

View 2

This view shows a very limited area, unless a winter scene without leaf mass where a pedestrian connection can be shown in full view

View 3

This one shows the entrance from the street only, therefore it will not be a good choice for the main illustration

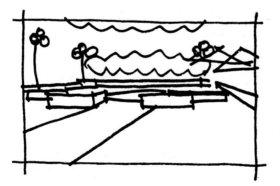

View 4

A sketch of this view will show most of the area and express the depth, distance and has room to show activities in the multi-purpose space

Fig. 4.2 ***Project No. 1,*** *Step 2, view selection, use thumbnail sketches to determine the view point you want to emphasize*

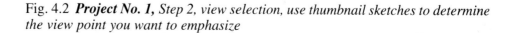

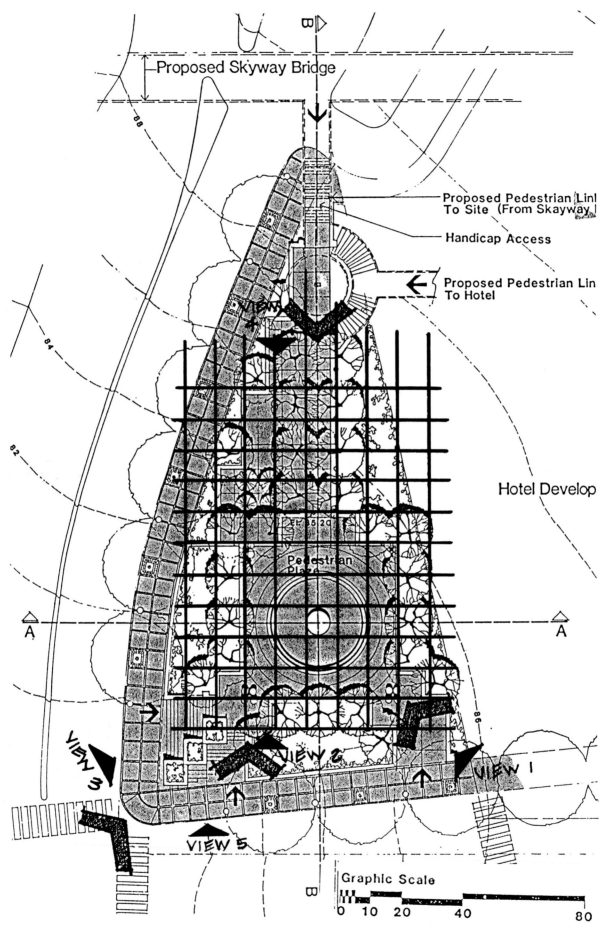

Fig. 4.3 *Project No. 1,* Step 3, place ten foot grids on the site plan, cover the area
to be shown in your illustrations, and select the view point(s)

126

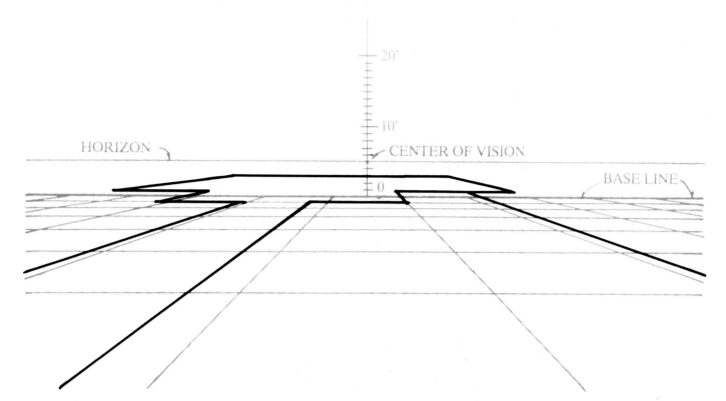

Fig. 4.4 **Project No. 1,** *Step 4, from the ten foot grid on the site plan, transfer the essential lines and points to the one-point perspective chart. Plot the outline of the area to be illustrated. Check the overall area. A rough size of the illustration can be determined at this time.*

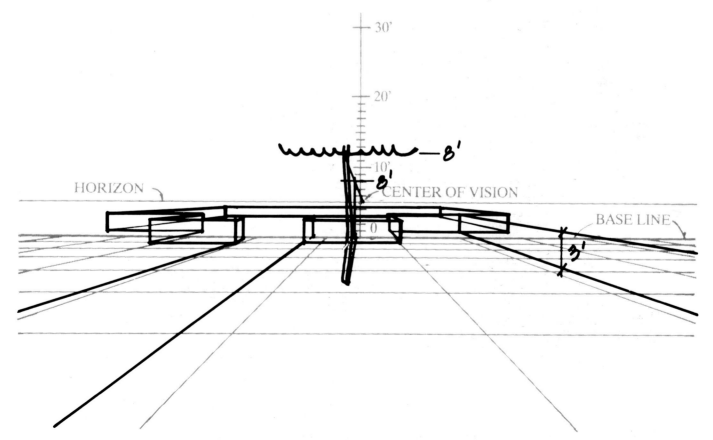

Fig. 4.5 **Project No. 1,** *Step 5, erect the height of the elements. Remember, the measurements always start from the Base Line. This is the most common mistake beginners usually make.*

127

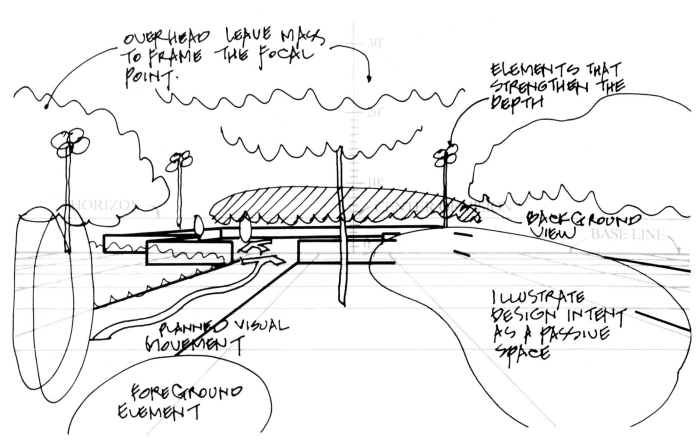

Fig. 4.6 *Project No. 1, Step 6, study the placement of the various elements*

Fig. 4.7 *Project No. 1, Step 7, plan the shadow areas to add three dimensional effects to the perspective. Sun angle should be in the range from the southeast to the southwest; select angle that is best for the illustration*

Fig. 4.8 *Project No. 1,* Step 8, finish the ink line drawing

Fig. 4.9 *Project No. 1,* Step 9, add shadows to line drawing using Zip-a-tone

Fig. 4.10 **Project No. 1,** *Step 10, color the finish drawing with color pencils on watercolor paper. Original size: 8" x 16"*

Fig. 4.11 **Project No. 1,** *finish sketch of view No. 2. Original size: 18" x 10 1/2"*

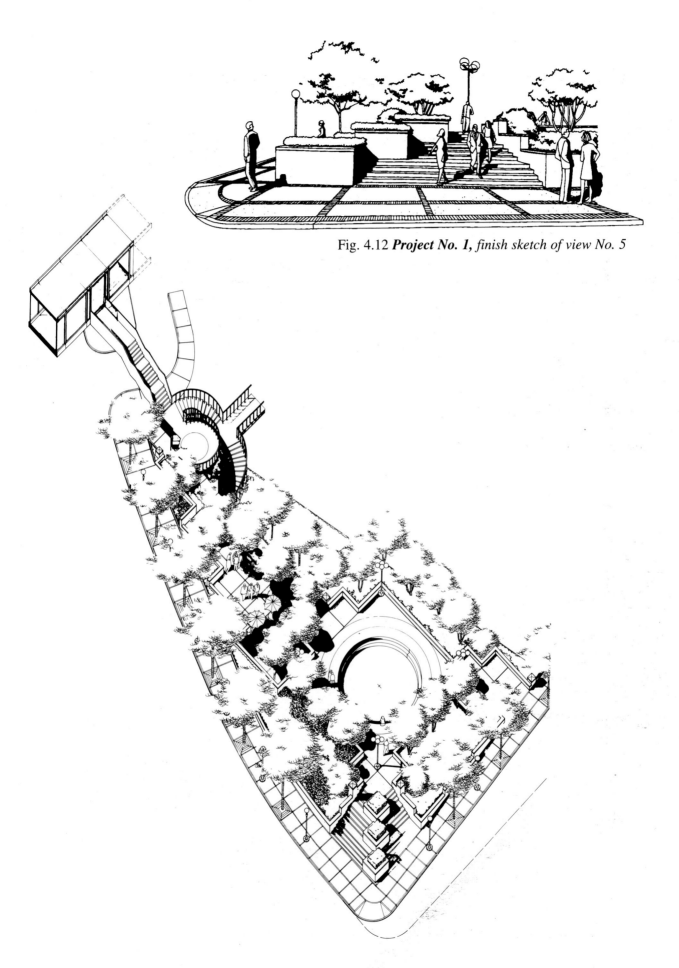

Fig. 4.12 **Project No. 1,** *finish sketch of view No. 5*

Fig. 4.13 **Project No. 1,** *finish axonometric view of the site. Original size: 28" x 40"*

131

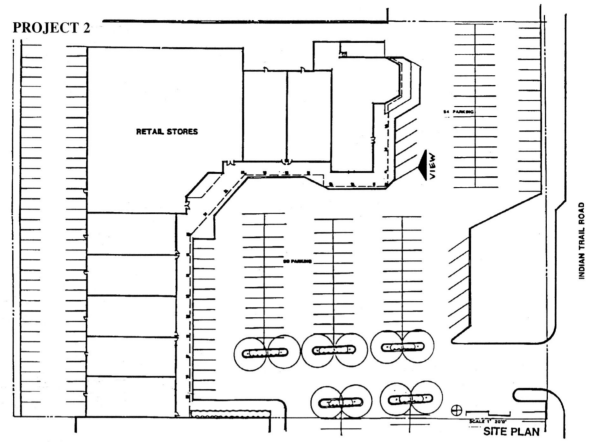

Fig. 4.14 *Project No. 2,* Step 1, secure a site plan of the project and select view point

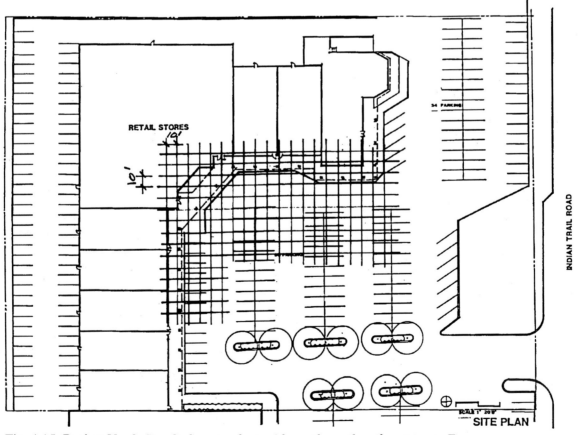

Fig. 4.15 *Project No. 2,* Step 2, draw ten foot grids north-south and east-west. For convenience, select a curb line to start the grid.

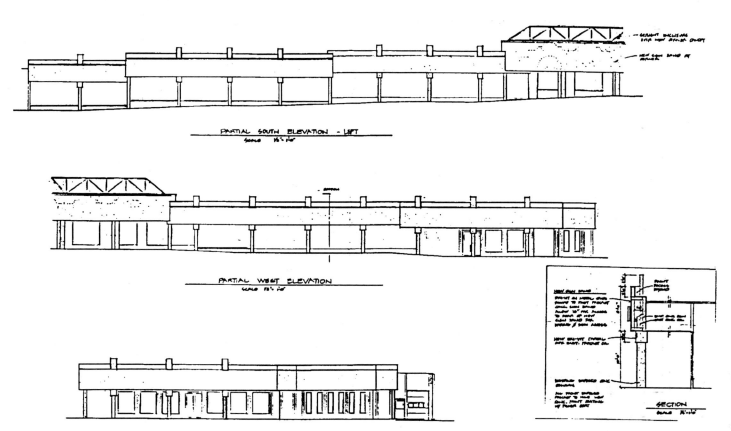

Fig. 4.16 *Project No. 2,* Step 3, secure the architectural elevations and sections

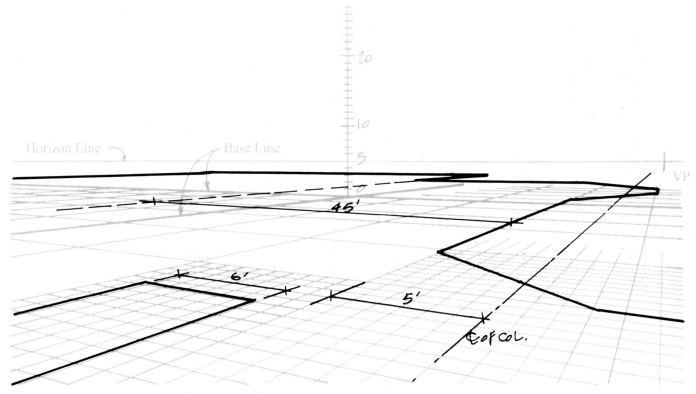

Fig. 4.17 *Project No. 2,* Step 4, plot the curb line and position the perspective format on the perspective chart. Position the focal point on the right to capture the "L" shaped shopping area.

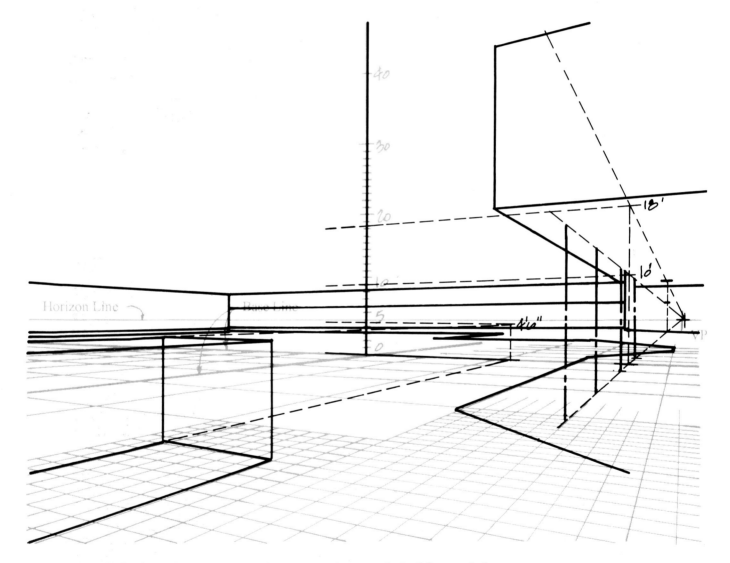

Fig. 4.18 *Project No. 2,* Step 5, at the same scale erect the building and element heights from the two vanishing points

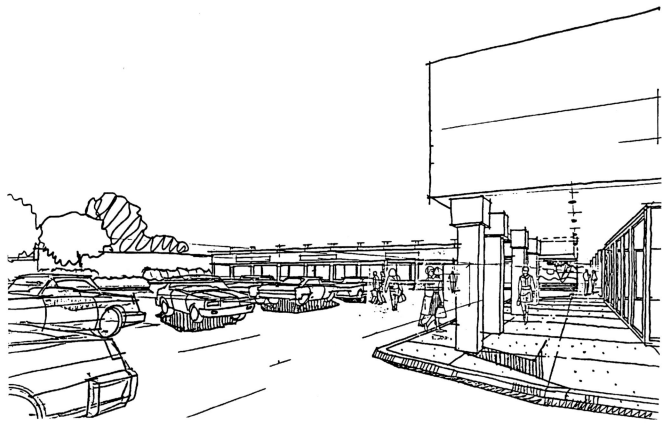

Fig. 4.19 **Project No. 2,** *Step 6, study the various elements and begin to detail them*

Fig. 4.20 **Project No. 2,** *Step 7, finished ink line perspective. Original size: 12 1/2" x 20 1/2"*

135

PROJECT 3

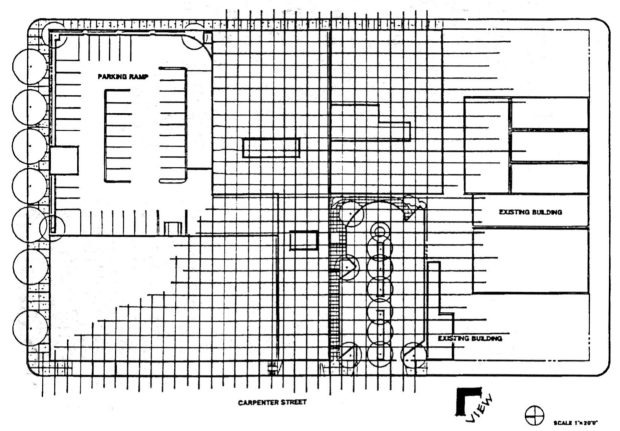

Fig. 4.21 *Project No. 3,* Step 1, secure site plan, draw ten foot grids on it, and select viewpoint

Fig. 4.22 *Project No. 3,* Step 2, photograph the existing building from various angles

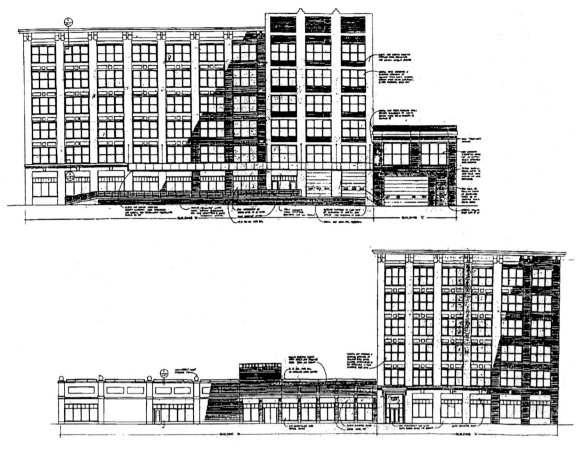

Fig. 4.23 *Project No. 3,* Step 3, obtain the proposed building elevations

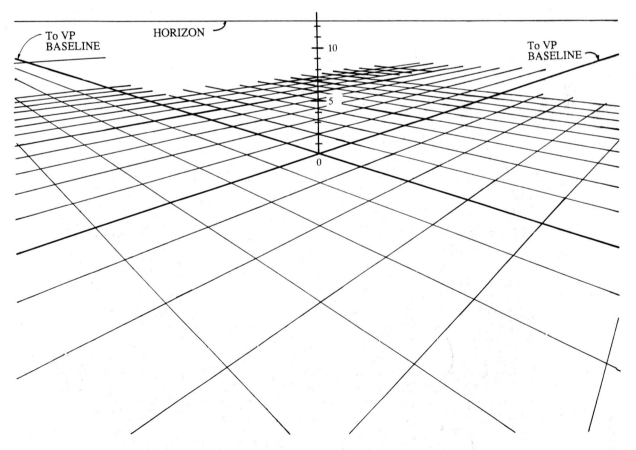

Fig. 4.24 *Project No. 3,* Step 4, using Lawson Chart #1 draw horizon line at 12'6"

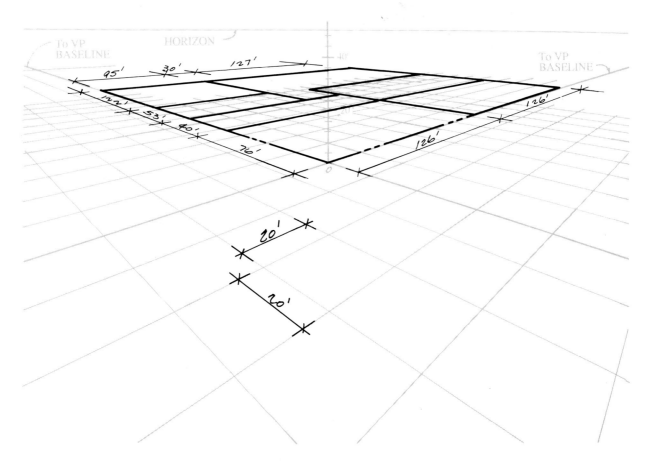

Fig. 4.25 *Project No. 3,* Step 5, reducing the scale four times, the horizon line then will be at 50'. Position the focal point at the center of the drawing and plot the property at the "0'" level.

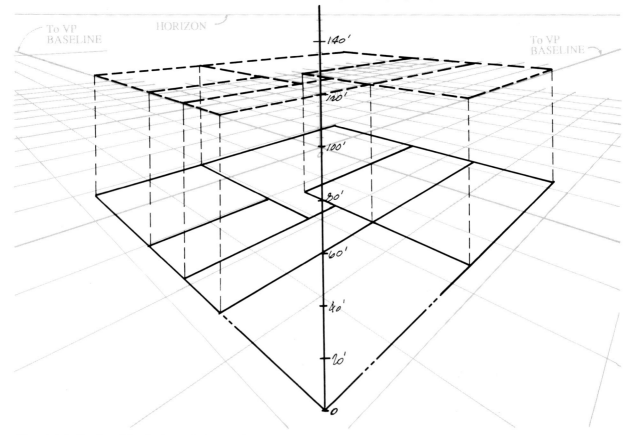

Fig. 4.26, *Project No. 3,* Step 6, lower the ground plan by 100 feet and plot the entire property and building outline at the new ground level

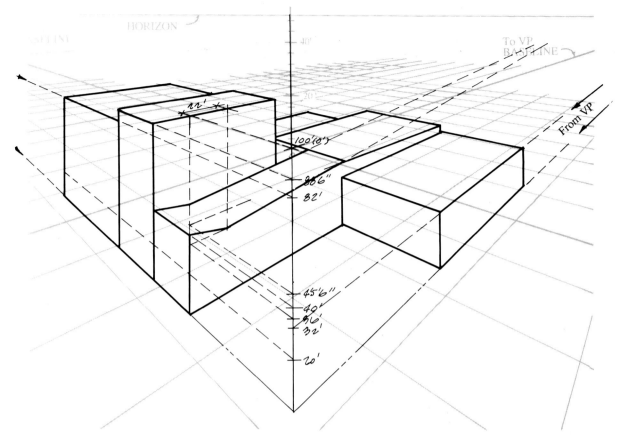

Fig. 4.27 *Project No. 3,* *Step 7, erect the heights based upon the reduced scale to form the blocks of buildings. Carry the horizontal dimensions from the original ground plan.*

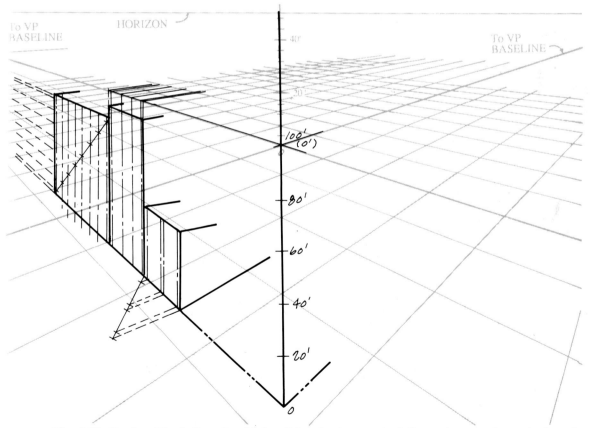

Fig. 4.28 *Project No. 3,* *Step 8, add detail by plotting vertical dimensions as shown in Step 6. Horizontal dimensions can be carried from the original ground plan, or by division methods as shown in Section 1.*

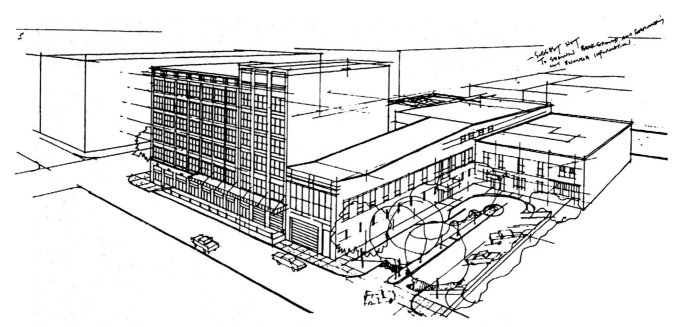

Fig. 4.29 *Project No. 3,* Step 9, rough layout with details

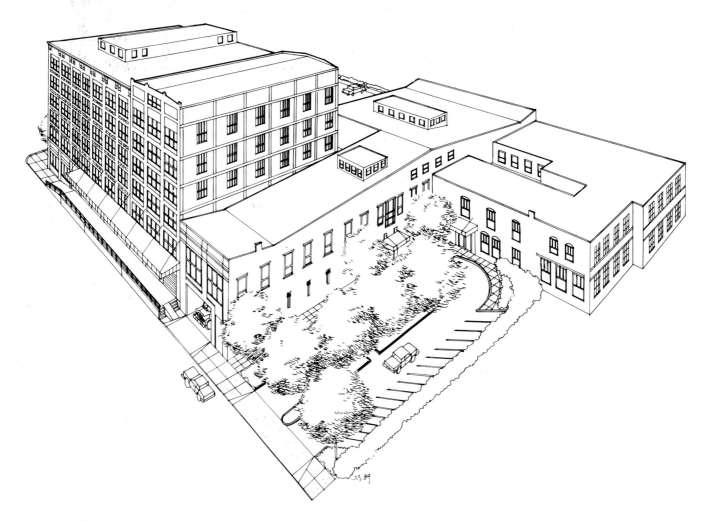

Fig. 4.30 *Project No.3,* Step 10, finished ink drawing. Original size: 16" x 21"

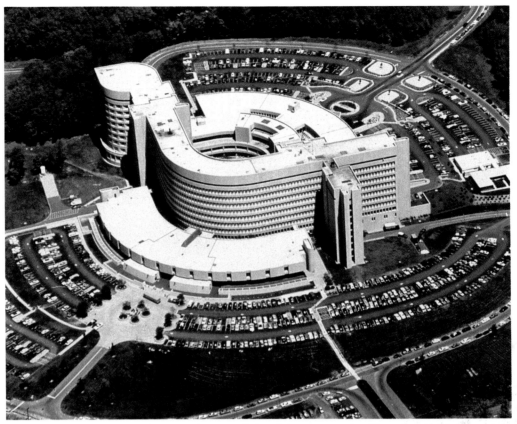

Fig. 4.31 *Project No. 4,* Step 1, obtain a slide of the existing building from which you can construct the addition

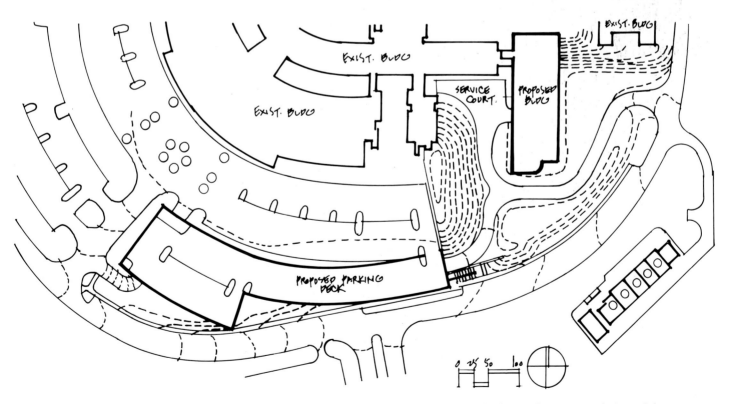

Fig. 4.32 *Project No. 4,* Step 2, secure a site plan which shows the proposed size of the building addition

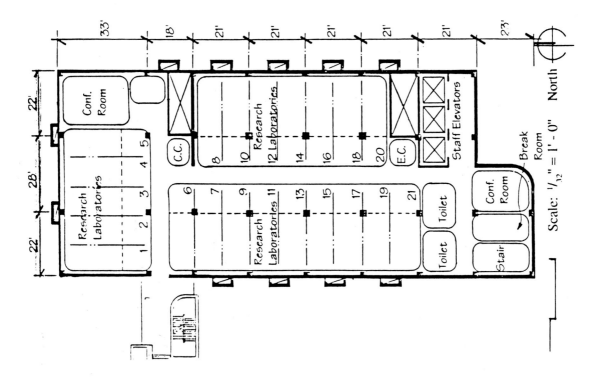

Fig. 4.33 *Project No. 4,* Step 3, use a floor plan which dimensions the building addition

Fig. 4.34 *Project No. 4,* Step 4, construct the building addition perspective using the same vanishing points as the existing building

142

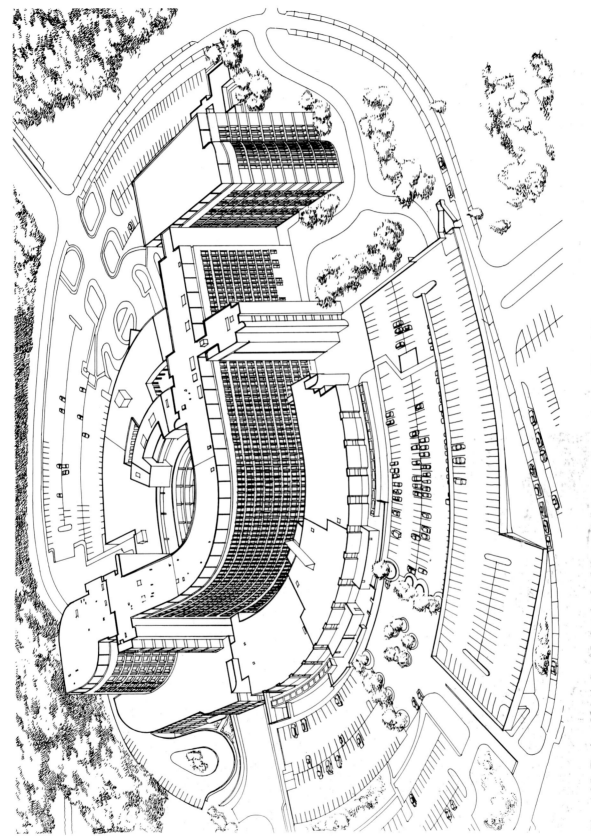

Fig. 4.35 *Project No. 4*, *Step 5, finished ink line perspective. Original size: 18" x 24"*

Fig. 4.36 *Project No. 4, Step 6, finished color perspective using markers on a black line print from Step 5*

144

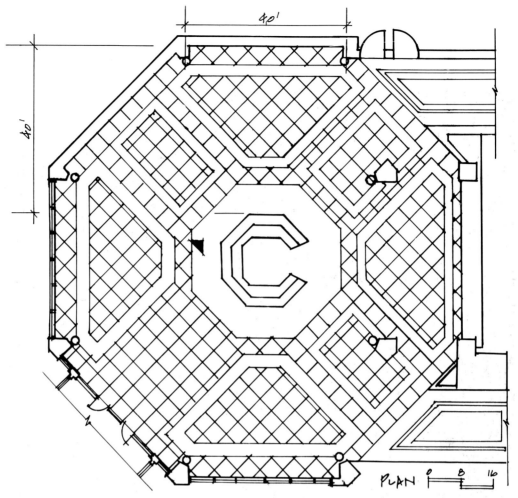

Fig. 4.37 *Project No. 5, Step 1, draw floor plan to 1/16" scale*

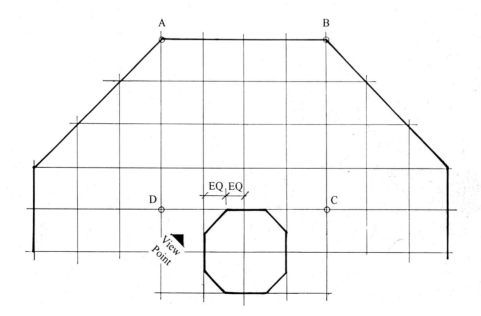

Fig. 4.38 *Project No. 5, Step 2, draw ten foot grid lines on plan and select view point*

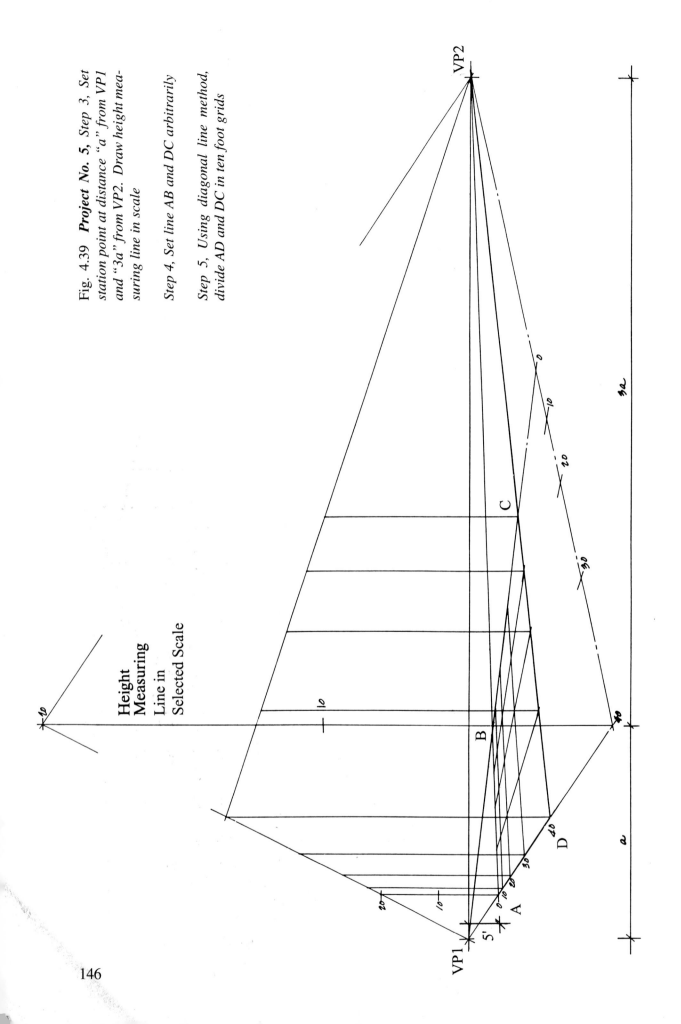

Fig. 4.39 **Project No. 5**, Step 3, Set station point at distance "a" from VP1 and "3a" from VP2. Draw height measuring line in scale

Step 4, Set line AB and DC arbitrarily

Step 5, Using diagonal line method, divide AD and DC in ten foot grids

Height
Measuring
Line in
Selected Scale

146

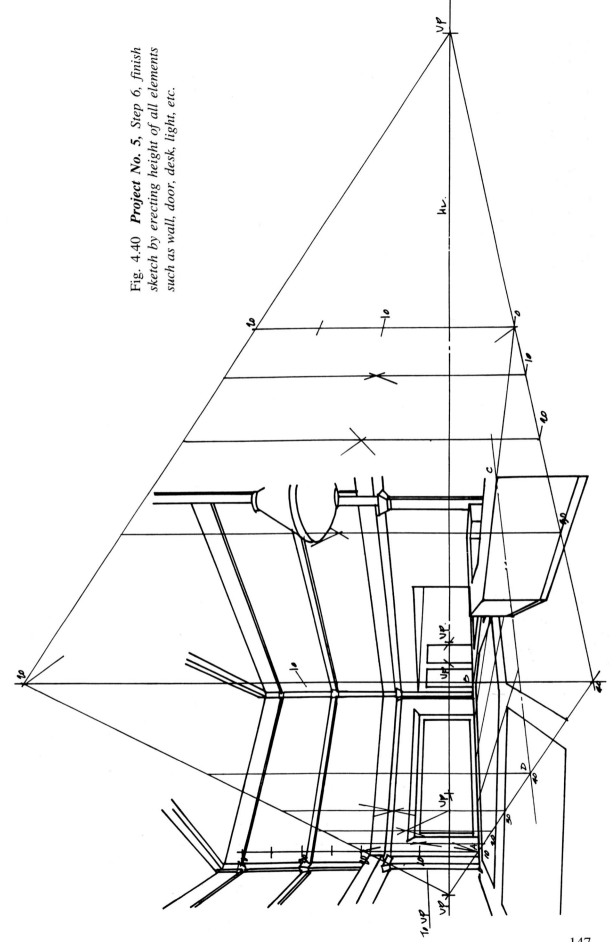

Fig. 4.40 *Project No. 5, Step 6, finish sketch by erecting height of all elements such as wall, door, desk, light, etc.*

147

5

EXAMPLES of
FINISHED ILLUSTRATIONS

In this section you will find a considerable range of perspectives. The projects vary in scale, technique, media and the degree to which they were finished. Some are rough sketches for a quick view of the design while others are highly finished for presentation to a corporate Board of Directors or City Council. In some cases there are several sketches for a project where the presentation need required or the budget allowed their development.

Fig. 5.1 *River Oak Shopping Center. Marker on black line print (top). Ink line on tracing paper (bottom). Original size 18" x 42"*

149

Fig. 5.2a *Design competition. Ink line on tracing paper, zip-a-tone added to bottom illustration. Original size: (top left) 24" x 24", (top right) 18" x 18", (bottom) 18" x 18"*

Fig. 5.2b *Design competition. Ink line on tracing paper. Original size (top)
16" x 32", (bottom) 18" x 30"*

151

Fig. 5.3 *Yanbu New Town, Saudi Arabia. Ink line and zip-a-tone*

152

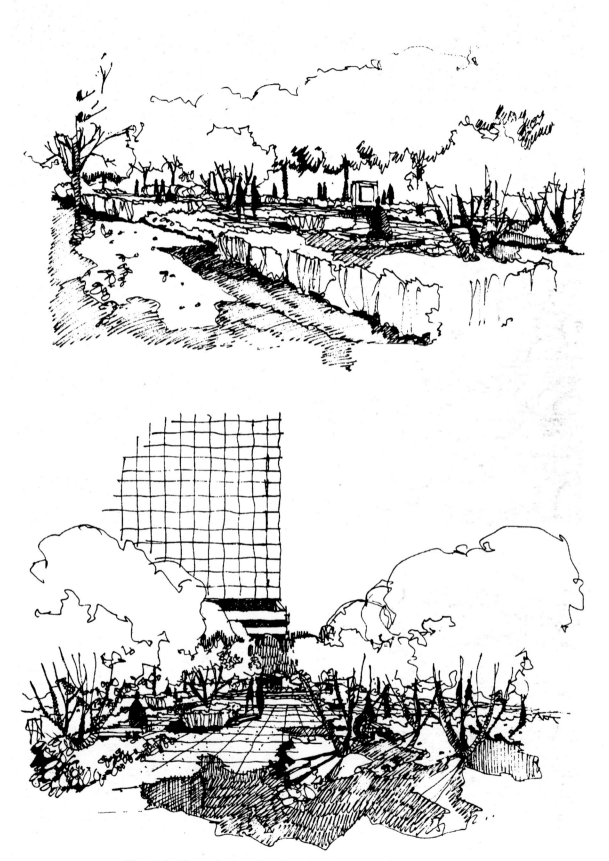

Fig. 5.4 *Plaza design sketches. Felt-tip pen on tracing paper. Original size
(top) 18" x 25", (bottom) 15" x 21"*

153

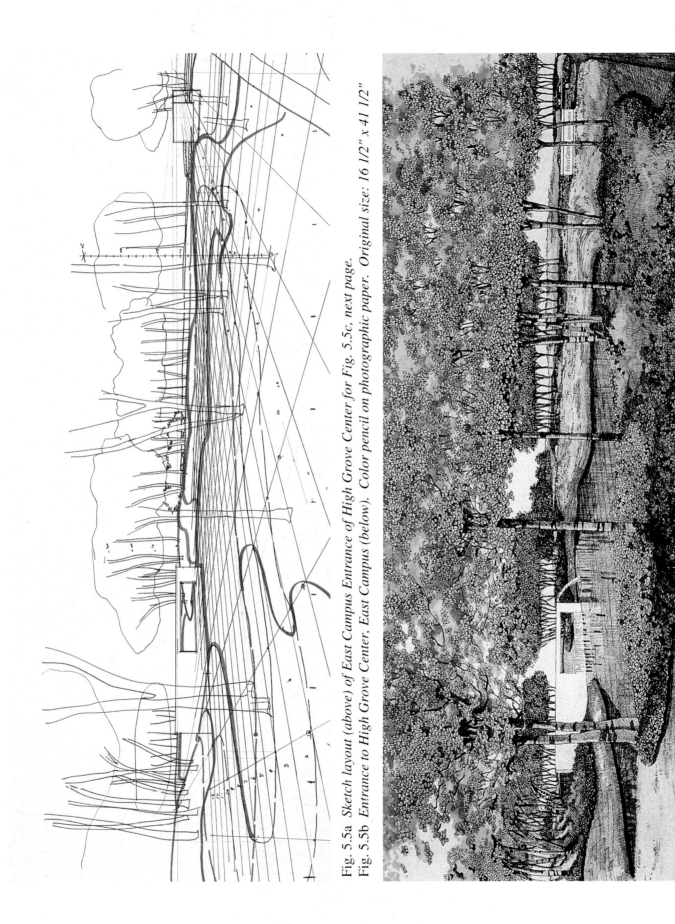

Fig. 5.5a *Sketch layout (above) of East Campus Entrance of High Grove Center for Fig. 5.5c, next page.*
Fig. 5.5b *Entrance to High Grove Center, East Campus (below). Color pencil on photographic paper. Original size: 16 1/2" x 41 1/2"*

Fig. 5.5c *Entrance to High Grove Center, East Campus. Ink line on mylar. Original size: 16 1/2" x 41 1/2"*

155

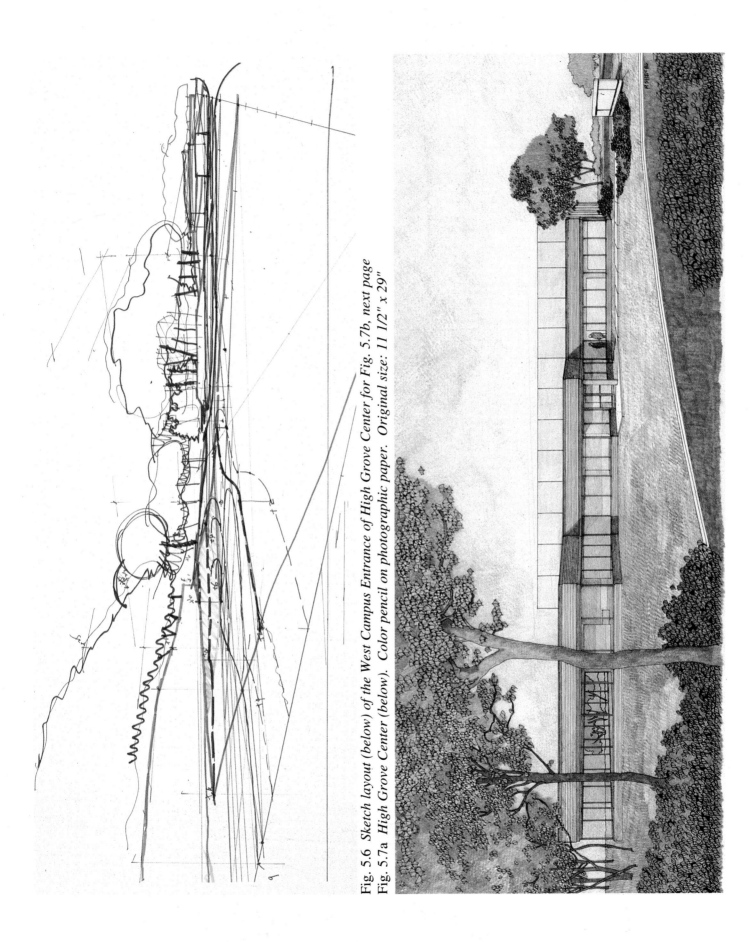

Fig. 5.6 Sketch layout (below) of the West Campus Entrance of High Grove Center for Fig. 5.7b, next page
Fig. 5.7a High Grove Center (below). Color pencil on photographic paper. Original size: 11 1/2" x 29"

Fig. 5.7b *High Grove Center West Campus Entrance. Ink line on mylar. Original size: 16 1/2" x 41 1/2"*

157

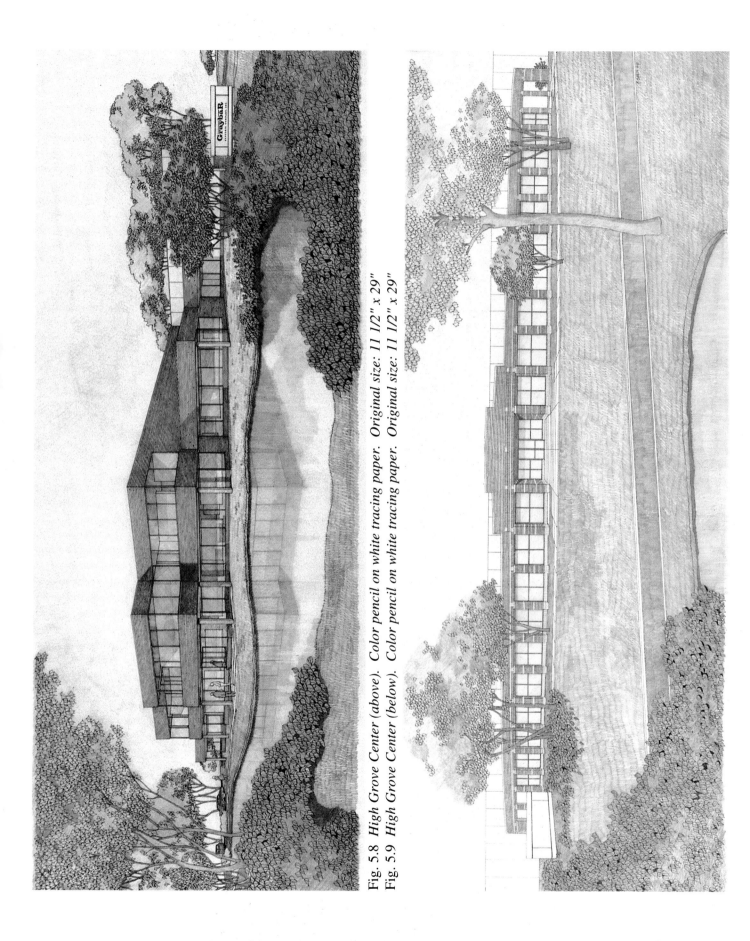

Fig. 5.8 *High Grove Center (above).* *Color pencil on white tracing paper. Original size: 11 1/2" x 29"*
Fig. 5.9 *High Grove Center (below).* *Color pencil on white tracing paper. Original size: 11 1/2" x 29"*

Fig. 5.10 *High Grove Center. Ink line on mylar. Original size: 11 1/2" x 29"*

159

Fig. 5.11 *Brooks Residence. Design stage sketches on tracing paper. Felt-tip pen and colored with Prismacolor pencil. Original sizes: 18" x 24"*

Fig. 5.12 *Brooks Residence. Ink line on mylar. Original size: as shown*

Fig. 5.13 *A residence. Pencil on mylar (top) and ink line on tracing paper (bottom). Original sizes: 5 1/2" x 7 1/2"*

162

Fig. 5.14 *A residence. Ink line on tracing paper. Original size: 18" x 30"*

163

Fig. 5.15 *McMahon Residence. Felt-tip pen with color pencil on tracing paper. Original size: 12" x 14"*

Fig. 5.16 *Mudd Memorial Roof Garden. Marker on black line print. Original size: 20" x 30"*

164

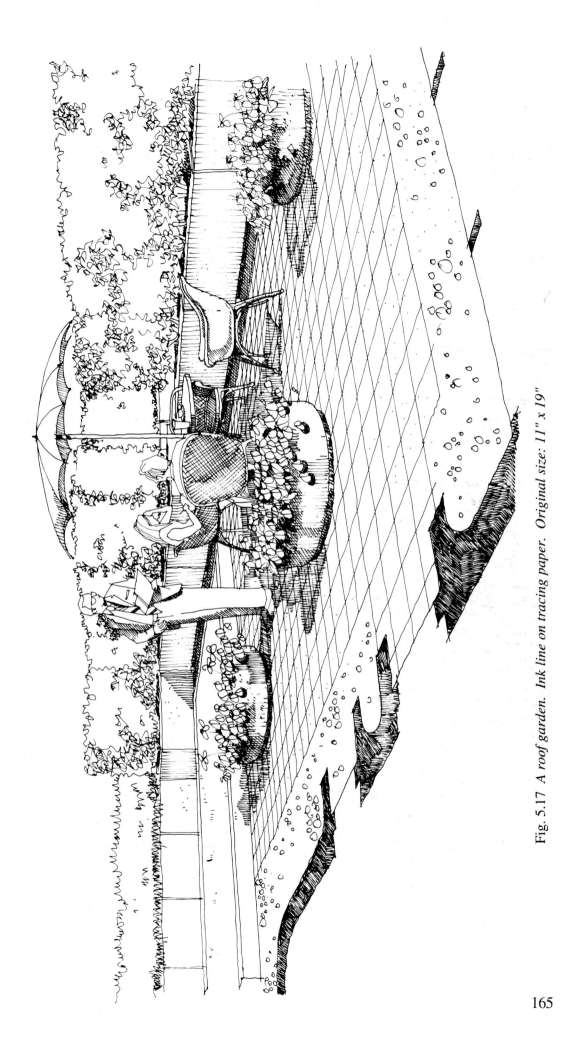

Fig. 5.17 *A roof garden. Ink line on tracing paper. Original size: 11" x 19"*

165

Fig. 5.18   *Sketch for a park.   Ink line on tracing paper.   Original size: 10" x 70"*

Fig. 5.19   *Design sketch of a bicycle and pedestrian path for a housing development*

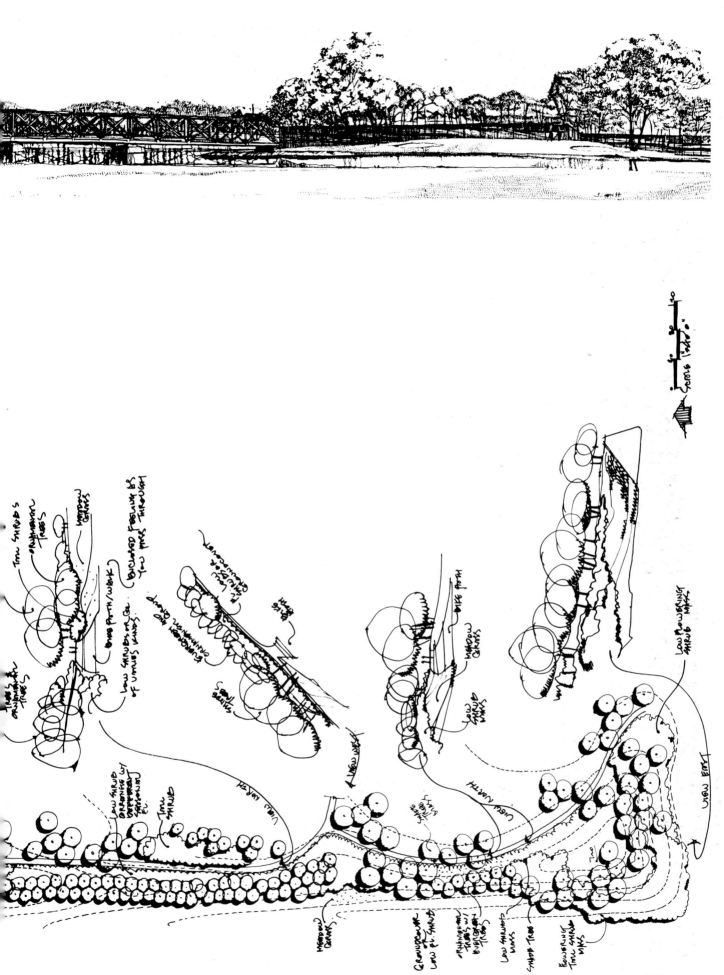

167

Fig. 5.20 *East Chicago Park System. Marker on tracing paper. Original sizes: 20" x 30"*

Fig. 5.21 *Lake Defiance State Park Entrance. Ink line on mylar. Original size: 24" x 28"*

Fig. 5.22 *University of Chicago Lab School play lot. Felt-tip pen on tracing paper. Original Size: 18" x 30"*

Fig. 5.23 A garden at a Presbyterian home. Felt-tip pen on tracing paper. Original size: 14" x 26"

Fig. 5.24 *John Hopkins University Research Building. Color pencil and freehand felt-tip pen on tracing paper. Original size: 18" x 24"*

Fig. 5.25 *John Hopkins University Research Building. Laboratory interior sketch. Color pencil and felt-tip pen on tracing paper. Original size: 16" x 28"*

Fig. 5.26 *John Hopkins University. Study sketch for composition and shadows. Original size: 24" x 24"*

172

Fig. 5.27 *John Hopkins University Court. Ink line on mylar. Original size: 14" x 24"*

173

Fig. 5.28 *John Hopkins University. Freehand sketch on tracing paper using felt-tip pen, color pencil and marker for a quick presentation.*

Fig. 5.29a *John Hopkins University. Watercolor on 140lb. cold press watercolor paper. Original size: 16" x 11"*

174

Fig. 5.29b *John Hopkins University. Ink line on mylar. Original size: 24" x 16"*   175

Fig. 5.30a *Promotional Sketch No. 1, Step 1, rough out.*

Fig. 5.30b *Promotional Sketch No. 1, Step 2, detail composition rough out*

176

Fig. 5.30c *Promotional Sketch No. 1, Finished ink line sketch on mylar. Original size: 28" x 28"*

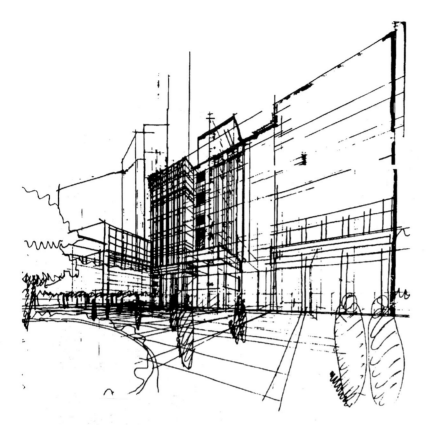

Fig. 5.31a *Promotional Sketch No. 2, Step 1, rough out*

Fig. 5.31b *Promotional Sketch No. 2, Detail composition rough
out*

178

Fig. 5.31c *Promotional Sketch No. 2, Finished ink line sketch on mylar. Original size: 28" x 28"*

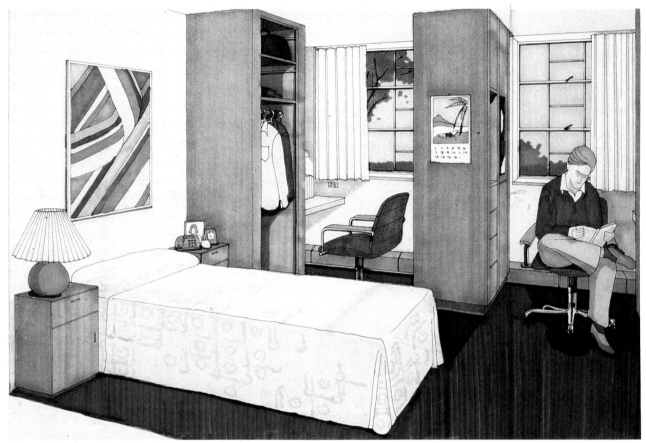

Fig. 5.32 *Osteopathic Health System Center. Marker on black line print. Original size: 18" x 24"*

Fig. 5.33a *Rush Presbyterian St. Luke Medical Center. Ink line drawing with color pencils on photographic paper. Original Size: 20" x 30"*

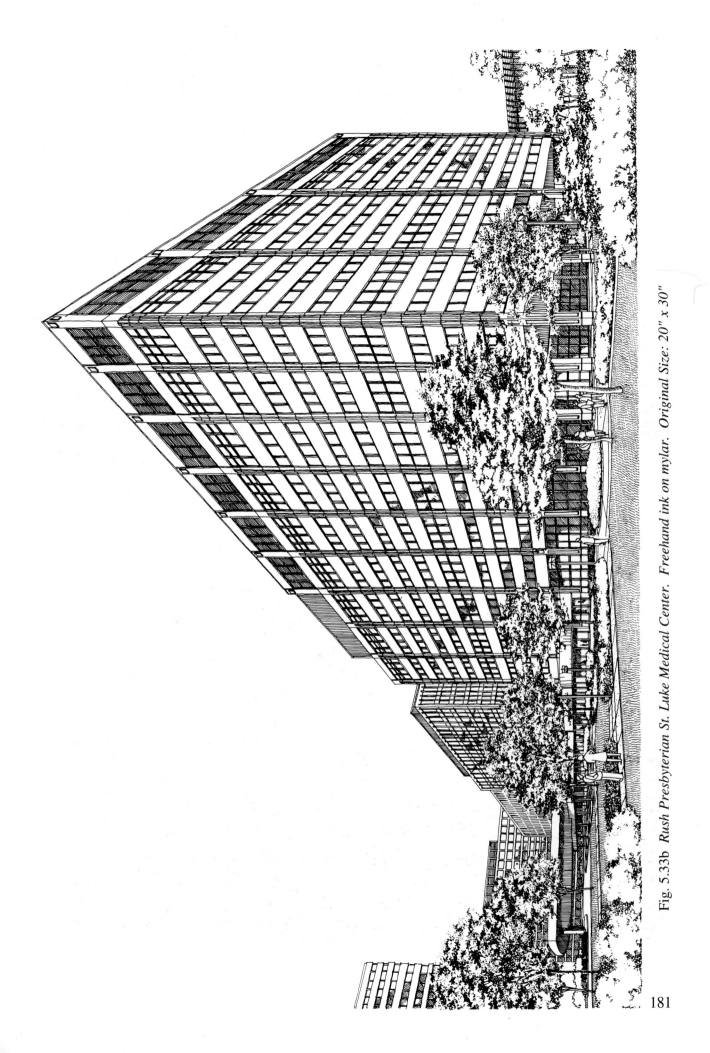

Fig. 5.33b Rush Presbyterian St. Luke Medical Center.   Freehand ink on mylar.   Original Size: 20" x 30"

181

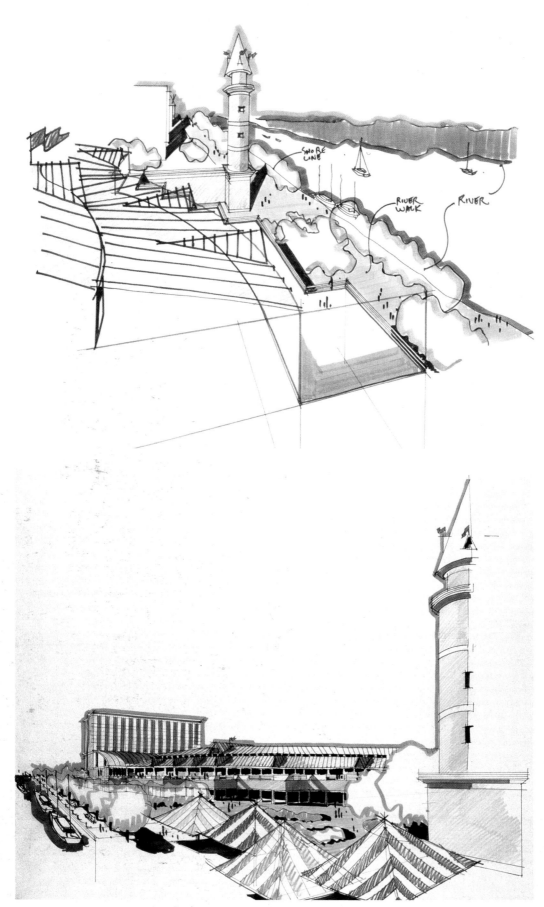

Fig. 5.34 *River Edge Plaza. Marker on white tracing paper. Original sizes: 30" x 36"*

Fig. 5.35 *Chicago Skyline. Freehand ink line on tracing paper. Original size: 12" x 12"*

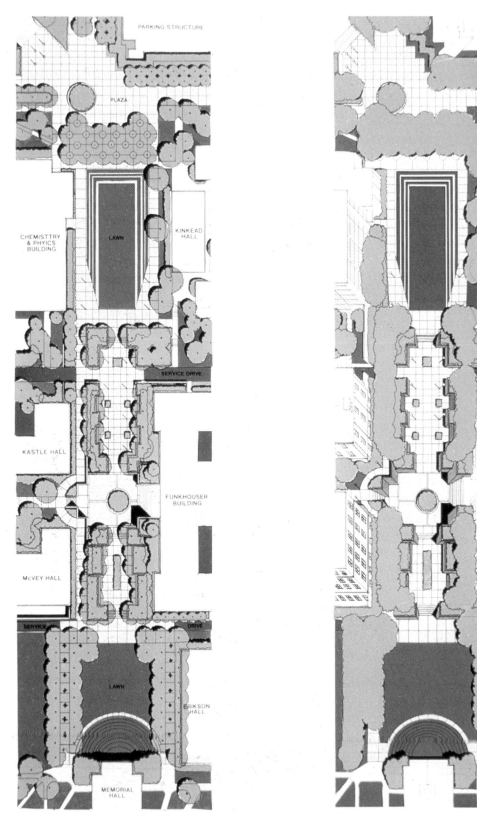

Fig. 5.36 *University of Kentucky Master Plan. Plaza Design, axonometric view. Penton transparent film on photographic paper base printed from a black line original drawing. Used as a refined presentation. Original size: 20" x 30"*

184

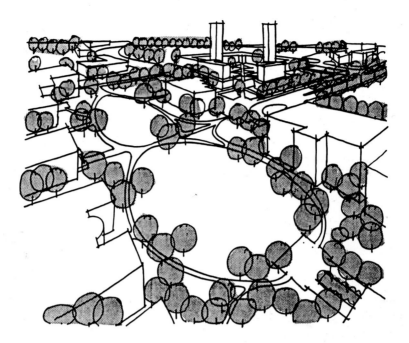

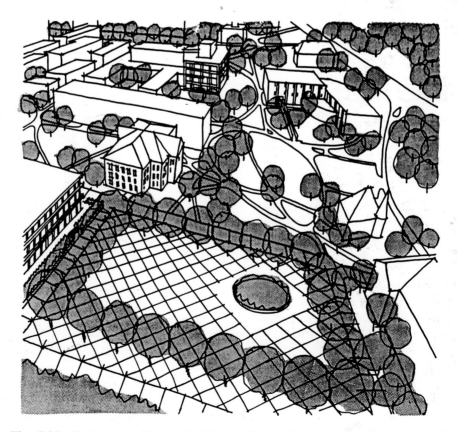

Fig. 5.37 *University of Kentucky Master Plan. Felt-tip on tracing paper with zip-a-tone. Original sizes: 8" x 8"*

185

Fig. 5.38 *A townhouse complex rendered with marker, except for airbrushed sky. Original size: 20" x 30"*

Fig. 5.39 *The First American Bank Plaza. Marker on black line print. Original size: 16" x 30"*

186

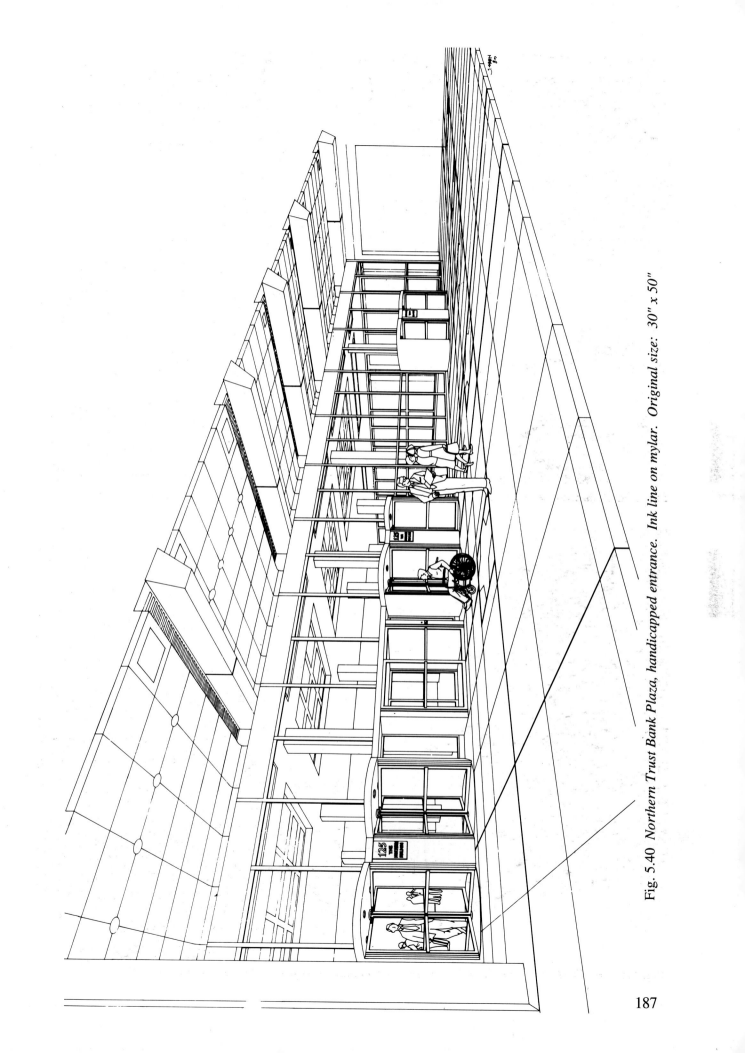

Fig. 5.40 *Northern Trust Bank Plaza, handicapped entrance. Ink line on mylar. Original size: 30" x 50"*

Fig. 5.41 North Avenue Toll Plaza. Color pencil on photographic paper (above). Ink line (below). Original size: 16" x 36"

Fig. 5.42 *Illinois Tollway. Ink line on mylar. Original size: 14" x 30"*

189

Fig. 5.43 *City of Harvey streetscape. Marker on black line print. Original size: 18" x 24"*

Fig. 5.44 *Highland Park Hospital Parkway design sketch. Felt-tip pen with marker on tracing paper. Original size: 12" x 30"*

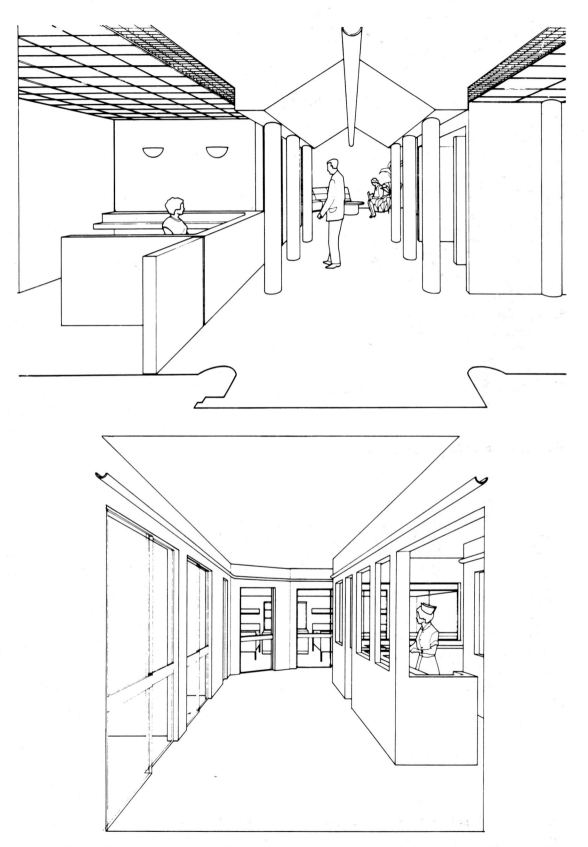

Fig. 5.45 *A hospital. Hardline ink line on mylar. Original sizes: 12" x 18" (top), 12" x 12" (bottom)*

Fig. 5.46a *1001 West Washington. Color pencil on photographic paper.*
Original sizes: 21 1/2" x 29 1/2"

192

Fig. 5.46b *1001 West Washington. Ink line on mylar. Original size: 21 1/2" x 29 1/2"*

Fig. 5.47 Evanston Technical Park Plaza. Ink line on mylar. Original size: 18" x 30"

194

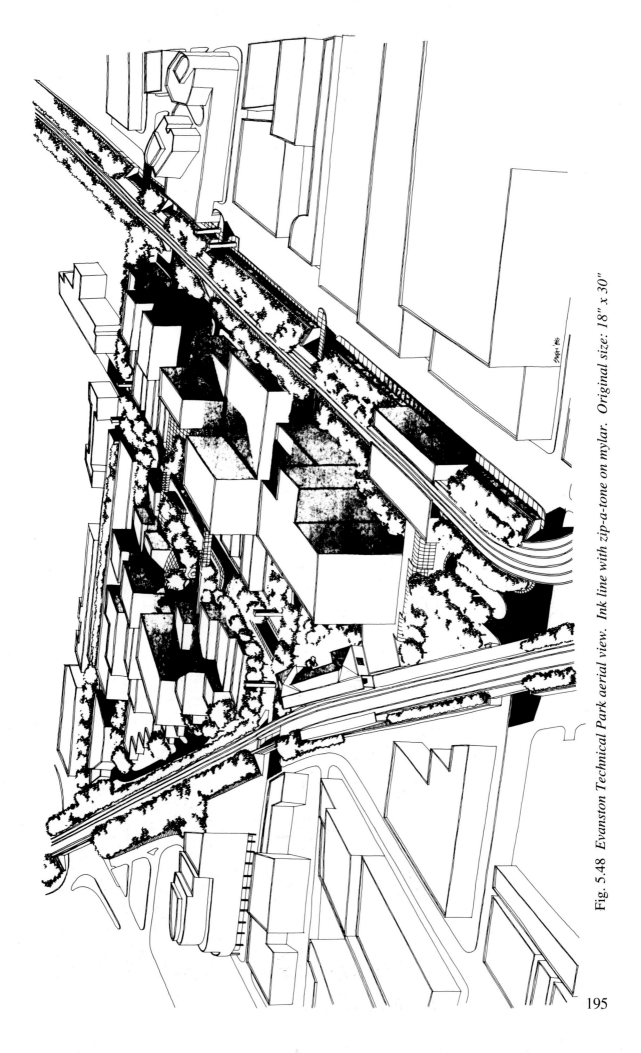

Fig. 5.48 *Evanston Technical Park aerial view. Ink line with zip-a-tone on mylar. Original size: 18" x 30"*

195

Fig. 5.49 *Abbott Laboratory Headquarters. Ink line on mylar. Original size: 21" x 30"*

196

Fig. 5.50 *Abbott Laboratory Headquarters.   Ink line on mylar.   Original size: 21" x 30"*

197

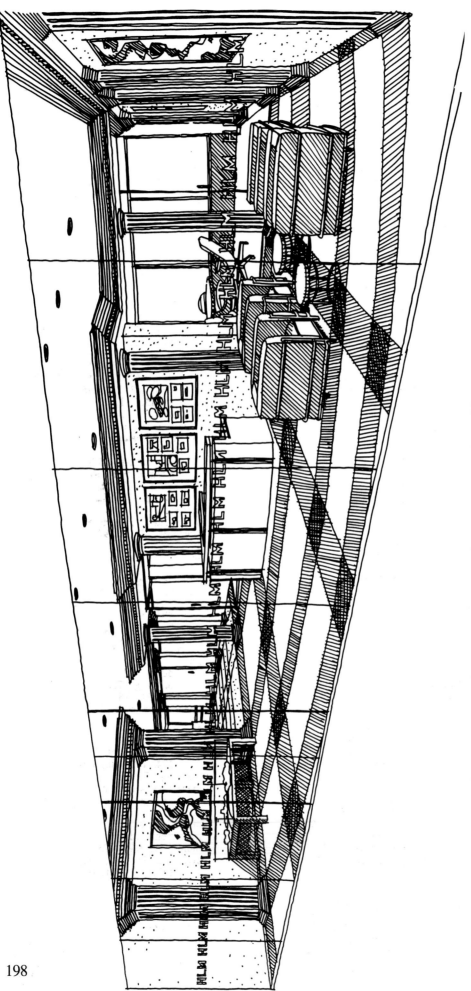

198

Fig. 5.51 *Hansen Lind Meyer Office Lobby. Freehand Pental. Original size: 20" x 30"*

Index

O

one-point perspective 15-16, 19, 31, 46, 51, 123
opaque medium 81
outlining 78
overhead plane 49
overlapping 74, 78, 83

P

painting 1, 79, 81-82
parallel 20, 28, 31, 54, 62
    lines 9-10, 24
pastel 81
    drawing 92
pavement 115
pedestrian 125
    path 166
    plaza 123
    ramp 64
pencil 79, 82, 160, 162
perpendicular 41, 54
perspective 15, 42, 82, 83, 123, 142
    chart 36-37, 127, 133
    construction 9, 38
    image 9, 13
    of steps 39
    projection 9
    theory 36, 93
    view 31, 113
photograph 78, 84-85, 109, 112, 136
photographic paper 2, 180, 184, 192
pictorial
    art 71
    plane 9
picture
    frame 109
    plane 9, 15, 20, 24, 28, 54
pigment 81
plan 20, 23-24, 28, 46
plane 9, 15
planter 61, 63, 83
plants 83, 85, 106, 109, 113
pleasant atmosphere 82, 84, 106
plexiglass 42
plot plan 2
point of emphasis 71-72
pond 70
practice 81
preplanning 1
principles of perspective 84
printing 79
project 1
projecting lines 10
projection 31
    lines 36
    method 36, 51
property 2, 138
proportion 2, 46, 95

R

reclining surface 60
rectangle 46
reduction 1
reflection 67
rendered finishes 105
rendering 78, 84-85, 115
repetition 74, 76, 113
reproduction 1-2
room 15, 20

S

scale 20, 23-24, 28, 31, 36, 41-42, 83-84, 107, 134, 139, 148
sculpture 68
sections 2, 8, 133
shade 79, 82, 84
    effects 114
shading 78, 83, 116
shadow 54, 116, 129, 172
    patterns 115
    of trees 66
shape 54, 74, 80
shrubs 83
side elevation 23, 28
site photos 2
site plan 2, 36, 42, 124, 127, 132, 136, 141
sky 80-82, 93
slides 83, 141
slope 62
snow 84
space 46, 77, 81, 83
splatters 80
spots 80
spray fix 79
square 31, 52
station point 9-10, 13, 15, 20, 24, 28, 42, 54
steps 2, 46, 51, 63
stipples 82
sun 54
symmetrical, 113

T

technique 2
tension 71
texture 72, 78, 80, 83-85, 106, 116-118
three dimension 2, 54, 82, 84, 128
three-point perspective 35
thumbnail sketches 125
time 1, 2, 42, 82
tissue paper 80, 82
tone 71, 78, 81
    drawing 87-88
tracing paper 151, 153, 160, 162, 164, 167, 168, 172, 174, 182-183, 185, 190
transparent wash 79
trees 2, 66, 69, 75, 83, 105-106, 110, 116
two-dimensional 9
two-point perspective 10, 25, 27, 46, 51, 123

U

understanding the drawing 41
unwanted detail 84

V

value 78
vanishing points 10, 15, 23-24, 36, 48, 52, 68, 85, 134, 142
vehicles 101-102
vellum 2, 79, 92, 99, 122

vertical
    dimensions 139
    frame 73
    height 42
    line 46
    measurement 24, 36, 49
    planes 53
    projection 15, 24
    site element 64
view
    path 71
    point 1, 24, 36, 67, 83, 125-126, 132, 145
viewer 9, 83
viewing
    angle 10, 31, 102
    distance 85
    heights 31
    location 24
vision line 15
visual
    interest 78
    judgment 46
    movement 74
    rays 9, 25
volume 78